The Selected Works of MAULANA ABUL KALAM AZAD

Volume - II
(1943-46)

Chief Editor

DR. RAVINDRA KUMAR

ATLANTIC

PUBLISHERS & DISTRIBUTORS (P) LTD

Published by

ATLANTIC

PUBLISHERS & DISTRIBUTORS (P) LTD

7/22, Ansari Road, Darya Ganj,
New Delhi-110002
Phones : +91-11-40775252, 23273880, 23275880, 23280451
Fax : +91-11-23285873
Web : www.atlanticbooks.com
E-mail : orders@atlanticbooks.com

Branch Office
5, Nallathambi Street, Wallajah Road,
Chennai-600002
Phones : +91-44-64611085, 32413319
E-mail : chennai@atlanticbooks.com

Printed in India at Glorious Printers, A-13, D.S.I.D.C., Jhilmil Industrial Area, Delhi-110095

To

MOTHER INDIA

Foreword

I am glad to write a Foreword to the Second Volume of the Selected Works of MAULANA ABUL KALAM AZAD (1943-46) edited by DR. RAVINDRA KUMAR, a distinguished scholar. He is a scholar who has brought out a number of authoritative works on several great sons of Mother India like Pandit Nehru, Sardar Patel, Netaji Subhash Bose and Vithalbhai Patel. He has been keenly interested in research works in various fields – Political Science, Philosophy and Indian History – and has devoted considerable amount of time and energy.

The present volume comprises of all correspondence, statements, speeches *etc.* of Maulana Azad from 1943 to 1946 which bring out certain ennobling aspects of his great and dedicated life.

Maulana Azad was a man of multi-dimensional personality. He is known as a great party leader and secularist. However, his contribution to a number of other equally important areas, during this period is not so known. This volume throw light on these areas also.

At a time when fissiparous tendencies are stalking the nation, broad based ideas of Maulana Azad, as contained in this Volume will provide impetus to the present generation for forging communal harmony.

I hereby congratulate DR. RAVINDRA KUMAR for the compilation of this work.

V.N. GADGIL

Preface

Dr. Shri Ravindra Kumar is an admirer of Maulana Abul Kalam Azad. This is nothing unusual. Maulana Azad had numerous admirers in the course of India's struggle for freedom. The number increased appreciably after India attained freedom. Partition of India was the heavy price India paid for this freedom. Maulana Azad had throughout his whole political life opposed forces which encouraged separatist trends in our national life. It was in the partitioned India that people realised more vividly the soundness of the views Maulana had expressed on the communal problem.

Maulana Azad was among the major figures in our unique struggle for freedom waged under the leadership of Gandhiji. The selected works which Dr. Ravindra Kumar has edited bring out the greatness of Maulana Azad in several fields of life. He was most assuredly an outstanding scholar, a great journalist, a matchless orator but with equal ease he was also a great statesman who played a significant role in every crisis which India and, in particular, the Indian National Congress faced from time to time in its struggle to make our country free and independent.

He had also his due share in shaping India's destiny in her first decade of Independence. He was an outstanding member of the union cabinet but what was more important was the mature advice he made available to his comrade and fellow warrior Pandit Jawaharlal Nehru as the latter sought to grapple with India's difficult and daunting problems in the first crucial phase of her independence.

Dr. Ravindra Kumar may not yet be a mature scholar but the enthusiasm he has shown in portraying the intellectual and political life of Maulana Azad deserves commendation. The country is still faced with problems which greatly exercised the Maulana's mind. What he thought and said on these problems would still be a source of inspiration and enlightenment to his countrymen in the difficult days through which we are all passing.

Sadiq Ali

Preface

Contents

Introduction

I

It gives me great pleasure to write Introduction to the second volume (1943-46) of the Selected Works of Maulana Abul Kalam Azad. He was staunch Muslim. But he stood for national unity and communal harmony as inevitable ingredients for newly born India as a nation. He made no difference between Hindu and Muslim and looked all kith and kin.

As it is known to all that during his tenure of six years (1940-46) as the President of Indian National Congress, Maulana Azad gave the organisation such a direction and programme which made its roots very firm. This six years period was of a great importance in the history of India and specially the period from 1943 to 1946 was very critical also. Wavell Plan, Cabinet Mission Plan, formation of Interim government in the Centre, under the Prime Ministership of Pandit Jawaharlal Nehru and the elections for the Legislative Assemblies in the provinces as well as in the centre etc. were some of the main events which took place during this time. Maulana Azad set up such ideas during this critical times that made Congress an eternal and peerless political organisation of the whole universe. In this volume, all important statements, extracts of speeches and talks, instructions, issued by Maulana Saheb and the Indian National Congress under his presidentship, have been incorporated. His correspondence with Sardar Vallabhbhai Patel in connection with the organisational matters is an important and interesting part of this volume (Document Nos. 35-37, 39, 40, 42-48, 52-53, 55, 57-60, 62-65, 72, 75-79, 81-87, 89). This part shows that for the cause of national interest they worked team-heartedly.

II

Another part of this volume second is the correspondence of Maulana Azad with the senior British official which shows his deep insight and well-matured understanding with which he corresponded with Lord Wavell, Pathick-Lawrence and Linlithgow (Doc. Nos. 1, 8, 10-14, 25, 26, 32, 49, 54, 71, 80, 93-99, 101-109, 111, 112, 114-121).

'Wavell Plan', 'Cabinet Mission Plan' and the question of political solution of India's future in 1946 were of great importance. The documents related to these questions are included here. Although the relation of the correspondence of Maulana Azad, during this period, is certainly with the British Official yet he made it clear through his letters that after the freedom of India there should be a communal unity, all must get due share and no one should suffer from injustice. To quote an example from his letter to Pathick-Lawrence on May 6, 1946 (Document 96), "We do accept the proposal for parity as between groups in regard to the executive or legislature. We realise that everything possible should be done to remove fears and suspicions from the mind of every group and community."

To Maulana Abul Kalam Azad all Hindus, Muslims, Sikhs and others were equal. He never tolerated injustice to any one. On the question of representation of the Hindus in the Cabinet and the constitution-maker Committee, the letter written by him to the Viceroy, Lord Wavell, make it clear.

To quote an example from his letter of June, 13, 1946 (Document 104) "these tentative suggestions emphasise the principle of 'Parity' to which we have been and are entirely opposed. In composition of the Cabinet suggested by you, there is parity between the Hindus including the Scheduled Castes and the Muslim League, that is the number of caste Hindus is actually less than the nominees of Muslim League. the present proposal thus puts the Hindus in a very unfair position and at the same time eliminate the non-League Muslims". Not only this but many other letters (Document Nos. 105 and 106, 111-116) expressed Maulana's clear views on the matter.

Document No. 1 of this volume is related to the letter which he wrote to Lord Linlithgow, the then Viceroy, in 1943 from the prison. This letter clarify that he was a true representative of Indian People.

He was also a true representative of Indian cultural heritage. In fact, Maulana Saheb was a staunch supporter of united India and was an advocate of cultural unity. In 1940, Horace J. Alexander wrote about him, ... "The present President of Indian National Congress, Abul Kalam Azad, who is a true and orthodox Muslim, with his many Hindu and Muslim friends, has been making afforts to scrape difference between the two main communities (Hindus and Muslims) of his country. His aim is to show that the Congress never want, as most of the people believe, majority has got – all its power."

Really, he thought the interest of all without any discrimination. It is also clear from his letter dated 09.07.1945, written to Master Tara Singh. He strongly opposed the demand of such a community that wanted more than its due. To quote one more example from his letter dated 14.06.1946 (No. 116) written to the Viceroy Lord Wavell, "The Sikhs in Punjab and Frontier Province will feel injustice by your plan and being in minority they are helpless." Again he said strongly, "On the cost of non-Muslims it is wrong to give representation in the Constituent Assembly to the undeserved people."

III

Thus the Second Volume will throw light on the great personality of Maulana Saheb on the one hand, it will add to the contemporary social, political and historical stock on the other. The readers will get more knowledge about Maulana Azad's life and work. I hope the third volume of this series (1947-48) will be brought out soon.

IV

I am thankful to Maulana Azad Memorial Academy, Lucknow for co-operation and help. I appreciate the efforts of this academy in which there is the feeling of Hindu-Muslim unity, justice and human freedom. Interest of the academy in the publication of these volumes has encouraged me. Its Patron, His Holiness, Maulana Syed Abul Hasan Ali Nadvi, General Secretary, Mr. A.J. Jalali and Treasurer Mr. S.G. Mohiuddin have inspired me for which I am grateful to them.

I am thankful to all institutions and archives which helped me for this volume specially, Nehru Memorial Museum and Library, New Delhi, National Archives of India, New Delhi, Gandhi National Museum and Library, New Delhi, Sardar Vallabhbhai Patel Smarak Bhavan, Ahmedabad and Calcutta National Library.

I am grateful to Mr. Sadiq Ali, Mr. Z.R. Ansari, Mr. V.N. Gadgil, Dr. Hari Dev Sharma, Prof. K.L. Malik, Mrs. Meera Kapoor, Mrs. Manju Sehgal, Prof. Dr. Malti Malik, Mr. Achal Kumar Awasthi, Mrs. Kamlesh Ravindra Kumar, Dr. Akbar Ali Khan and Mr. Anil Kumar Juneja for their kind co-operation and help, in many ways, in the preparation of this volume.

RAVINDRA KUMAR

Abbreviations

A.D.	Akali Dal
A.I.C.C.	All India Congress Committee
A.I.C.P.B.	All India Congress Parliamentary Board
A.I.M.L.	All India Muslim League
A.I.S.A.	All India Spinners' Association
B.H.U.	Benaras Hindu University
B.G.K.U.	Bombay Girni Kamgar Union
B.P.C.C.	Bombay Provincial Congress Committee.
B.P.C.C.	Bihar Provincial Congress Committee
B.W.C.	British War Cabinet
C.D.	Civil Disobedience
C.D.M.	Civil Disobedience Movement
C.E.B.	Central Election Board
C.F.	Cripps' Formula
C.L.P.	Congress Legislative Party
C.M.P.	Cabinet Mission Plan
C.P.I.	Communist Party of India
C.O.	Congress Organisation
C.P.	Central Provinces
C.P.S.C.	Congress Parliamentary Sub-Committee
C.S.P.	Congress Socialist Party
C.W.C.	Congress Working Committee
D.R.C.	Delhi Resolution of the Congress
D.T.	Delhi Talk
F.D.I.N.C.	Foreign Department of Indian National Congress
G.B.	Government of Bengal
H.E.V.	His Excellency the Viceroy
H.M.G.	His Majesty's Government

I.N.C.	Indian National Congress
I.N.T.U.C.	Indian National Trade Union Congress
K.P.	Khadi Programme
L.R.M.L.	Lahore Resolution of Muslim League
M.C.L.P.	Madras Congress Legislative Party
M.L.A.	Member of Legislative Assembly
M.L.C.	Member of Legislative Council
N.G.	National Government
N.M.B.	Nationalist Muslim Board
N.P.C.	National Planning Committee
N.V.	Non-Violence
N.W.F.P.	North West Frontier Province
P.C.C.	Provincial Congress Committee
P.G.	Provincial Government
P.S.V.	Private Secretary to the Viceroy
R.F.	Rajaji Formula
S.A.D.	Shiromini Akali Dal
S.D.P.S.P.	Sanatan Dharam Pratinidhi Sabha of Punjab
S.G.P.C.	Shiromini Gurudawara Prabandhak Committee
U P.P.C.C.	United Provinces Provincial Congress Committee
V.E.C.	Viceroy's Executive Council
V.H.	Viceroy's House

List of Documents

Contd.

Contd.

No.	Subject	Date
49.	From Wavell	29.10.1945
50.	From Jawaharlal Nehru	31.10.1945
51.	From Mahatama Gandhi	01.11.1945
52.	From Vallabhbhai Patel	06.11.1945
53.	To Vallabhbhai Patel	06.11.1945
54.	To Wavell	07.11.1945
55.	From Vallabhbhai Patel	11.11.1945
56.	From Nehru and Patel	12.11.1945
57.	To Vallabhbhai Patel	12.11.1945
58.	From Vallabhbhai Patel	12.11.1945
59.	From Vallabhbhai Patel	13.11.1945
60.	To Vallabhbhai Patel	13.11.1945
61.	To J.B. Kripalani	15.11.1945
62.	From Vallabhbhai Patel	15.11.1945
63.	To Vallabhbhai Patel	15.11.1945
64.	From Vallabhbhai Patel	15.11.1945
65.	From Vallabhbhai Patel	24.11.1945
66.	To Rajendra Prasad	25.11.1945
67.	From Jawaharlal Nehru	27.11.1945
68.	To Rajgopalachari	27.11.1945
69.	To Rajgopalachari	10.12.1945
70.	The Congress Manifisto for Central and the Provincial Elections with Maulana Azad as President	11.12.1945
71.	From Lawrence	21.12.1945
72.	From Vallabhbhai Patel	21.12.1945
73.	From Jawaharlal Nehru	1945
74.	Congress Working Committee's Resolution on Indonesia with Maulana Azad as President	1945

Contd.

Contd.

Contd.

Document No. 1

LETTER FROM MAULANA AZAD TO LORD LINLITHGOW

13.02.1943

Dear Lord Linlithgow,

My colleagues and I have read in yesterday's and day before yesterday's newspapers the recent correspondence that had passed between you and Mahatma Gandhi[1]. In the course of your letter to Mahatma Gandhi numerous references have been made to the Congress, repeated and far reaching charges have been made against the Congress Organization. In your letter of January 13, you express your regret that no word of condonation for the violence and crime should have come from the Working Committee.

Ordinarily we would refrain from saying anything while we are kept in detention cut off completely from our people and the outside world. Even our place of detention is supposed to be a secret which may not be mentioned or whispered to any one. Our sources of information here are strictly limited and consist only of some newspapers which under existing rules and ordinances publish only censored news and are prohibited from giving publicity to many facts of news which are of vital importance to us and to the Indian people. In the circumstances it is obviously improper for us to give expression to any views in relation to events with which we are ill-acquainted, especially when the only method of doing so open to us is to address the Government of India.

I wish to confine myself more especially to one issue and to make it clear that so far as we are concerned both as individuals and in our corporate speaking on behalf of our organization, your charge that the Congress had organised a secret movement of violence is wholly false and without foundation.

As an English Patriot and a lover of British freedom, it should not be possible for you to appreciate how Indian patriots and lovers of India's freedom might feel and it should be possible for some element of fair-play and square dealing to be kept up in our relation to each other. To make serious charges against those who are prevented from replying to them, to make these charges (without producing evidence to support them) by the vast propaganda machine of a powerful Government and at the same time to supply news and views which are contrary to them are not evidence either of fair-play or a strong case.

In your letter of February 5, you say you have amply information that the campaign of sabotage has been conducted under secret instructions circulated in the name of the All India Congress Committee. What your information is we do not know. But we do know and can state with authority that the All India Congress Committee at no time contemplated such a campaign and never issued such instructions secret or...other. The A.I.C.C. was declared an unlawful association at the time of our arrest and practically all prominent and responsible Congressmen including the members of A.I.C.C. were arrested. At the same time the A.I.C.C. Office and other Congress officers were seized by the Police. Since then the A.I.C.C. cannot obviously function.

You mention that an underground Congress Organization exists now and that the wife of a member of the Congress Working Committee[2] is a member of it. We know nothing of such an organization and are not in a position to find out. We are convinced that no Congress Organization and no responsible Congressmen or Congress-men can be actually engaged in planning the bomb outrages and other acts of terrorism.

Congressmen no doubt consider it their duty to carry on civil resistance under certain circumstances to the best of their ability. But this has nothing in common with the charge you have made. It is possible that in the mind of the average official or policemen there is no particular difference between Civil disobedience and bomb outrages, etc., but we have no doubt in our mind, knowing our people as we do, that responsible Congressmen cannot possibly encourage in any way bomb outrages and terroristic acts.

A great deal is said about secret organizations, evidence of which the Government claims to possess but which it does not produce. May I draw your attention to the public speeches delivered by Mahatma Gandhi at the last meeting of the A.I.C.C. on August 8,[3] a few hours before his arrest wherein emphasised with all solemnity his appeal for non-violence. The Congress adopted this polity of non-violence 23 years ago and despite popular lapses occasionally, has not with a great measure of success in regard to it.

This will be evident from a comparison of the Indian National Movement with national movements in other countries which have often based themselves upon violence. You have no doubt yourself approved of violence in many forms when you have considered that it was used for right cause. The Congress, however, has adhered to its creed and practice of non-violence and has for these 23 years preached this method of the people. It the Congress decides to change its policy and method and function in this matter like other national Organizations, it would do so openly and deliberately by changing its creed to that effect. There would be no secrecy, for apart from other valid reasons a conflict between public and secret advice stultify any organization which is based essentially on open action and constructive endeavour.

The Congress may have many faults but it has not been accused of lack of courage in the pursuit of its objectives and ideals.

I would suggest to you to consider what the result in India might have been if the Congress had deliberately instigated and encouraged violence and sabotages since the Congress is widespread and influential enough to have produced a situation a hundred times worse than anything that has so far happened.

In the summer of 1940 when France fell and England was facing dire peril, Congress which had been previously thinking in terms of direct action, deliberately avoided this in spite of strong demand for it. It did so entirely because it did not want to take advantage of a critical international situation or to encourage Nazi aggression in any way. Nothing would have been easier than for the Congress during those critical days to produce a situation of the utmost embarrassment to the Government.

For many weeks prior to our arrest we had been pointing out in Working Committee Meetings, resolutions and otherwise, that public feeling in the country had grown exceedingly better against the British Government in India. Not only we, but many moderate leaders stated publicly that they had never previously know such bitterness. Responsible Congressmen tried to divert this feeling into peaceful channels and largely succeded in doing so. They would have succeeded even more if events had not taken place which suddenly exasperated the public and at the same time removed all prominent and well-known leaders who might have been able to control the situation. These events are better known to you than to us, situated as we are; but we have learnt enough to realise what the shock to the public must have been wholesale arrests were followed immediately by the prohibition and prevention of all public activity and all public expressions of opinion, by lathi charges, tear gas, bombs and shooting, well-known leaders spirited away and their destinations were kept secret. Rumours of death and illness spread and added to the public excitement was the background of the happenings during the second week of August last.

I do not wish to deal here with subsequent events for their adequate consideration requires further knowledge than we possess here but I would like you to consider what the effect on the Indian people must have been of all that has been done to them on behalf of the Government since our arrest and how large numbers of people must have been driven to desperation.

Reference has been made in the Government communique accompanying the recent published correspondence to a certain circular which is said to have been issued by the Andhra Provincial Congress Committee. We know nothing of this and cannot believe that improper instructions against the fundamental principle of the Congress could have been issued by any responsible Congress authority.

It is worthy of note, however, that even official reference to this circular contradict themselves. The first mention of it was made in a press note issued by the Government of Madras on August 20. In this it was stated that the Circular contained instructions *inter alia* for the removal of rails. Two weeks later Mr. Amery speaking in House of Commons stated that the circular expressly said that rails should not be removed and that there should be no danger to life. This is an instructive and significant instance of how evidence is made up and used to influence people.

In your letter of February 5 in referring to the A.I.C.C. Resolution you draw attention to the concluding part in it which authorises Congressman to set for themselves in the event of interference with the leadership of the movement. This has appeared significant to you and you have drawn certain conclusions from it. You are evidently unaware that similar instructions were given when previous Civil Disobedience Movement (of 1940-41) was started. In the individual Civil Disobedience Movement of 1940-41 these instruction were repeated by me on many occasions. It is of the essence of Civil Disobedience or Satyagraha that individual should become self-sufficient units, should need...as leaders are always likely to be removed and isolated at an early stage. In the present instance, the phase of Civil Disobedience was not reached.

It is curious that in a fairly lengthy correspondence and in various official statements nothing is said about the minutes of the resolution passed by the A.I.C.C., which dealt with the national and international situation and made it clear that a free India would not only resist invasion to the utmost but would throw all her resources into the world struggle for freedom and align herself with the United Nations. This was made perfectly clear in resolution itself. It was further emphasised by me speaking as president and by many other speakers.

It must be known to you that ever since the early beginning of Fascist, Japanese and Nazi aggression in Africa, Asia and Europe, the Congress has consistently condemned them. No organization in India or elsewhere has been so clear and emphatic on this subject.

The A.I.C.C. Resolution of August last was especially based upon the ante-Axis policy and in particular of the urgent necessity of strengthening India's defence against invasion. It was made clear and I emphasised it on that occasion that an acid test of the change was this defence of India and ... the strengthening of the United Nations. It may also be known to you that several members of the present British Government have in the past repeatedly supported or welcomed fascism and Japanese aggression.

You conclude your letter to Mahatma Gandhi by saying that the charges against the Congress will have to be met sooner or later. We shall welcome that day when we can face the people of the world and leave the verdict to them. On that day others also including the British Government will have to meet and answer charges. I trust they will also welcome that day.

Yours sincerely,
Abul Kalam Azad

His Excellency,
Lord Linlithgow,
The Viceroy's House,
New Delhi

---

1. See appendices (120-130)
2. Aruna Asaf Ali, wife of Mr. Asaf Ali, a member of A.I.C.C.
3. Speech of Gandhiji in Bombay in which he had declared famous Quit India Movement.

Document No. 2

LETTER FROM THE PRESIDENT OF S.A.D. TO MAULANA AZAD

15th March, 1943

Sir,

It is now certain that Sir Stafford Cripps is coming to make an effort to settle the problem of Indian SWARAJ. This appears to be a genuine effort and may prove to be a final one. It is also clear that Sir Stafford Cripps will try to settle the Communal Problem in India. So I wish to remind you that the Congress gave a promise to the Sikhs in 1929 by a resolution passed in the Annual Session held at Lahore that the Congress would be no Party to any Communal settlement which would not satisfy the minorities including the Sikhs. I, therefore, suggest that in order to avoid any misunderstanding and to remove misapprehensions, some Sikhs representing the Sikh Community may be consulted at every stage of the Communal Settlement.

I am,
Your most obedient servant,
President,
Shiromani Akali Dal & Shiromani Gurdwara
Parbandhak Committee

To,
Maulana Abul Kalam Azad,
The President
The All India Congress Committee, Calcutta

Document No. 3

TELEGRAM FROM MAULANA AZAD TO LORD WAVELL

BIRLA HOUSE
21.6.1945

LORD WAVELL
VICEROYS CAMP,

CONGRESS WORKING COMMITTEE AUTHORISES ME TO ACCEPT YOUR INVITATION TO SIMLA CONFERENCE ON TWENTY-FIFTH STOP HOPE REACH SIMLA TWENTY-FOURTH STOP WOULD BE GRATEFUL IF YOU CAN CONVENIENTLY SEE ME BEFORE CONFERENCE STOP THANKFULLY ACCEPT OFFER ACCOMMODATION TWO SECRETARIES ACCOMPANYING ME

ABU KALAM AZAD

Document No. 4

EXPRESS TELEGRAM FROM MAULANA AZAD TO DR. KHAN SAHIB

BIRLA HOUSE
21.6.45

DR. KHAN SAHIB
PESHAWAR,

PLEASE ATTEND CONFERENCE AT SIMLA TWENTY-FIFTH STOP IF POSSIBLE MEET ME THERE. TWENTY-FOURTH FOR FURTHER INSTRUCTIONS.

ABU KALAM AZAD

Document No. 5

CONFIDENTIAL (23.6.1945)

INSTRUCTIONS TO CONGRESSMEN, FROM THE PRESIDENT[1] ATTENDING SIMLA CONFERENCE ON JUNE 25, 1945

1. It must be clearly understood that the suggested arrangements are being considered on an interim and temporary basis only, and especially in regard to communal parity. The principle of such parity is neither acceptable nor desirable. It is an evil when and if accepted in the Centre and cannot be extended to the Provinces.

2. While communal parity in the limited and temporary sense may be agreed to, it must be clearly understood that this does not mean that all the Muslim members of the National government will be nominated by or consist solely of the Muslim League. The Congress cannot recognise the sole right of such nomination by a communal organisation; nor can it reduce itself as a consequence to a limited communal field. The Congress, therefore, is of opinion that names may be proposed for Hindus including Scheduled Classes, Muslims, etc., by all groups in the Conference to be adopted by the Conference as a whole.

3. While the Working Committee is anxious to help in finding a way out of the present deadlock which leads to Indian freedom and will work to that end, it must be remembered that any decision taken by it and even acted upon has to be confirmed and ratified by the A.I.C.C. The fact that the A.I.C.C. and other Congress Committees are still banned is an obstacle in our way and must be regarded as coercion.

4. Further the fact of large numbers of Congress prisoners must interfere with the progress of the Conference.

5. Clarification to be sought from the Viceroy or in the Conference in regard to:

(i) External Affairs Department.

(ii) Financial implications of defence.

(iii) How far it is possible to give a nationalist character to the Indian Army without at present changing its status or organization in any way. The Indian Army – officers and men – should have the same freedom of meeting people as the British Army has in England. The present barriers isolating them to go.

(iv) Allied victory in South-East Asia must mean freedom of the countries concerned, from all Imperialist control, British or other. Prohibition of the use of Indian resources for the deprivation of freedom of any other countries must be an accepted fact.

(v) In regard to the Indian States while recognising that during the interim period, the powers of the Crown Representative continue, it is clear that the national government will have to deal with many matters which overlap and have concern with the states in regard to trade, industry, labour, treatment of the people in the states etc. The Government will, when it considers this necessary, make suggestions and recommendations in regard to other State matters to the Crown Representative. Further that barriers between the states people, Princes and members of the national government and their associates should be removed so as to help in mutual discussion and consultation and the consideration of common problems, thus leading to the solution of these problems and even amalgamation with Federal India.

(vi) Provincial coalitions would depend on the particular conditions of parties and groups in each particular provinces.

(vii) The question of recruitment for higher services and the commitments made in regard to them must be reviewed. Commitments in regard to foreign recruitments cannot be accepted, though the national government will, whenever, it considers it necessary, welcome and engage foreign experts.

Note – The President will add to these, matters requiring elucidation, whenever he considers this necessary and give such other directions as may be required. He may also make such alternations as he considers necessary.

1. Maulana Abul Kalam Azad.

Document No. 6

TELEGRAM FROM MAULANA AZAD TO JAWAHARLAL NEHRU

1.7.45

THE WORKING COMMITTEE ADVISES YOU TO RETURN TO DELHI, AS PROMISED, TOMORROW. THE WORKING COMMITTEE'S FIXED DISCUSSION AWAITS YOUR RETURN. I HAVE ASKED H.H. THE MAHARAJA OF KASHMIR TO ADJOURN SHEIKH ABDULLAH'S CASE.

Document No. 7

TELEGRAM FROM JAWAHARLAL NEHRU TO ABUL KALAM AZAD

2.7.45

YOUR MESSAGE CONVEYED TO ME, ALSO NEWS POSTPONEMENT SHEIKH ABDULLAH'S TRIAL TO JULY 1. IN VIEW GRAVE DISCOURTESY OFFERED TO ME BY KASHMIR GOVERNMENT IN SPITE OF MY FRIENDLY APPROACHES, DEEPLY REGRET WHOLLY UNABLE RETURN UNTIL FULL LIBERTY OF MOVEMENT, INCLUDING VISIT TO SRINAGAR, ACCORDED TO ME. REQUEST WORKING COMMITTEE PROCEED WITHOUT ME.

JAWAHARLAL

Document No. 8

LETTER FROM MAULANA AZAD TO LORD WAVELL

Armsdell,
Simla, 7 July, 1945

Dear Lord Wavell,

1. On behalf of the Congress I am sending you a list of the names of the members of the proposed Executive Council, except for one name of a Sikh nominee, which I hope to send in a day or two. This list consists of both Congressmen and non-Congressmen and contains names for the entire Executive Council. According to this, the Council will consist of 15 members apart from His Excellency the Viceroy and His Excellency the Commander-in-Chief. We have felt that this is desirable at present in order to give representation to as many minority communities as possible. The Congress attaches special value to minority representation.

2. We have given a list of fifteen members and no more. My Committee have endeavoured to choose persons not for the honour the posts will give but for the burden they will entail. We have considered the whole question of assuming this responsibility from the point of view of its being a step positively in the direction of the independence of India, and we have observed that the British Government also consider it as such a step. For us, as also I hope, for you, Indian independence should involve the freedom of other nations hitherto under foreign rule and exploitation.

3. Regard being had to the conditions prevailing in the country, an endeavour has been made to make the list as inclusive as possible.

4. We have added three names of the leaders of the All India Muslim League but, of course, it is understood that the final choice in regard to these three names lies with the Muslim League. We have tried in the best way we can to contact the All India Muslim League as such but have failed.

5. You will note too that the list contains the name of the President of the Hindu Mahasabha. We have added his name without obtaining his previous permission.

6. It has given us particular pleasure to include in our list the name of a women, a member of a well-known Christian family and a leader of the women's movement in India.

7. The qualification we have sought in each case has been the greatest ability available, the common factor being independence as the immediate objective after the defeat of Japan.

8. One of the names included in the list is that of a present member of the Executive Council. We are strongly of opinion that in order to start anew, the old members of the Executive Council should not be included, but the name given belongs to a new member who is not associated with past policies.

9. My name has been included in the list, but, may I say, that it is only after the greatest hesitation and reluctance that I have agreed to my committee's direction in this matter. My colleagues felt that I must accept this responsibility. What has finally weighed with me is the fact that the post is one of duty.

10. It has not been possible for us to consult all those whose names have been suggested. In the event of any of those suggested being unable to serve, I trust you will allow us to submit alternative names.

11. The Committee have tried to enter into the spirit of the proposals. They have recognised in you the leader of the Conference in the best sense of the word – a designation carefully chosen by yourself. As you are at liberty to draw attention to any discrepancy you may detect in the list or any difficulty His Majesty's Government may feel, I need hardly assure you that it will be my Committee's best endeavour to accommodate you or His Majesty's Government. It is my earnest wish that you will not put an undue strain on my Committee by imposing any alteration in the list which you as leader will finally prepare before submitting it to the Conference.

12. I have added some brief particulars about the names on the list hereto attached.

Yours sincerely,
A.K. Azad

Lord Wavell,
Viceroy Lodge,
Simla

Document No. 9

LETTER FROM MAULANA AZAD TO MASTER TARA SINGH

Armsdell,
Simla, July 9, 1945

Dear Master Tara Singh,

Pandit Govind Ballabh Pant has told me of his conversations with Sardar Mangal Singh. There has been, and is, no question of any condition being imposed by or on the Congress. But it is common ground, as you told me yourself and as Pantji has assured me, that your cordial cooperation will be available in the great task of achieving Indian independence and advancing the welfare of the people of India.

We have therefore decided to include your name in the list sent by us to the Viceroy. Our list was sent on Saturday last to the Viceroy but at that time we left a vacancy in it and informed the Viceroy that we would add the name of a Sikh representative in a day or two. I am now writing to the Viceroy giving your name for this place and am informing you accordingly. So long as formal publicity is not given to the lists, any matter pertaining to them should of course be kept confidential.

Yours sincerely,
Abul Kalam Azad

Master Tara Singh,
Hotel Cecil,
Simla

Document No. 10

LETTER FROM LORD WAVELL TO MAULANA AZAD

Viceregal Lodge,
Simla, 13 July, 1945

Dear Maulana Saheb,

Thank you for your letter of 13th July. I am sorry if I did not make my position clear to you when I saw you yesterday. As you know, I intend to make a statement when the Conference meets tomorrow, and I hope this will make my position quite clear to you. In the meantime I am sure that you and your colleagues will attach no importance to the "authentic assertions" to which you refer towards the end of your letter. There will naturally be a great deal of irresponsible speculation, but it can certainly not be authentic, as I have not disclosed my selections, and do not inted to do so.

Yours sincerely,
Wavell

Maulana Abul Kalam Azad,
Armsdell,
Simla

Document No. 11

LETTER FROM MAULANA AZAD TO LORD WAVELL

Armsdell,
Simla,

13.7.1945

Dear Lord Wavell,

In my letter to you of July 7th forwarding a list of names on behalf of the Congress for the proposed Executive Council, I had suggested that you might draw our attention to any discrepancy in our list or any difficulty that His Majesty's Government may feel. I had hoped that this list as well as any other list or names contemplated by you would be discussed by you with me, and I had assured you that it would be my Committee's best endeavour to accommodate you. I was surprised, therefore, at the absence of any such consideration during our yesterday's conversation and at your non-disclosure of your list to me. I did not understand this then and do not even now understand it after discussion with my colleagues. You hesitated because you thought that your list might not be acceptable to my colleagues or me. It is not possible for me to say, without knowing the contents of the list, what our reaction to it would have been. But I feel that in thinking as you did you were less than fair to Congressmen who, on your own admission, had tried, in spite of heavy odds, to help you in every way possible. I should like to emphasise the fact that the whole of the Working Committee was released on the 16th June 1945 and your broadcast on the Conference was delivered on the previous day, June 14th. Further that many noted Congressmen and colleagues of ours are still under detention and the A.I.C.C. is still an illegal organisation. Because of long periods of imprisonment most of us are as yet hardly fit for strenuous work. Nevertheless, taking the proposals at their face value, Congressmen have responded to your invitation and rendered all possible help.

In the circumstances I suggest that you owe it to us to show you list and let my Committee have the option if they wish of rejecting it or suggesting modifications. At the Conference you had said that you would discuss your list with the leaders.

I may inform you that what are claimed to be authentic assertions are being made as to the contents of your list. They appear to be startling.

I feel, therefore, that you should show your list not only to me for being discussed with my colleagues but finally place it before the conference for adoption, unless on second thought you conclude that it must be withdrawn.

Yours sincerely,
A.K. Azad

Lord Wavell,
Viceregal Lodge,
Simla

Document No. 12

LETTER FROM MAULANA AZAD TO LORD WAVELL

Armsdell, Simla,
14 July, 1945

Dear Lord Wavell,

I was decided that the proceedings of the Leader's Conference should be kept confidential so that untimately or improper publicity may not in any way affect its decisions. Now that the Conference is over, there is no longer the same justification for keeping the transactions secret. On the contrary, such a course may lead to unauthorised speculations and misrepresentation of the attitude of the participants to the Conference. It is therefore, the desire of the Congress Working Committee that I should place before the public the attitude and the policy the Congress had maintained throughout the Conference, and publish the relevant correspondence in that connection. You will, I am sure, agree that the Congress owes it to its supporters as well as its critics to state and clarify the position it has adopted throughout the Conference. I trust you will have no objection to my doing so through the press.

Yours sincerely,
A.K. Azad

Lord Wavell,
Viceregal Lodge
Simla

Document No. 13

LETTER FROM LORD WAVELL TO MAULANA AZAD

Viceregal Lodge, Simla,

15 July, 1945

Dear Maulana Sahib,

Thank you for your letter of 14th July. I do not think that as Chairman of a Conference which has now dispersed, I can properly authorize any party or delegate to depart from the decision that the proceedings should be confidential. The decision was not intended to cover the period of the conference only – the idea was that the delegates would speak more freely if they knew that what they said was not going to be recorded or published.

I am not sure what the correspondence is to which you refer. If it includes the letter you sent me with your list of names, and the list of names itself you will remember that it was the particular wish of the conference that the lists sent to me by parties should not be disclosed.

Yours sincerely,
Wavell

Maulana A.K. Azad,
Simla

Document No. 14

LETTER FROM MAULANA AZAD TO LORD WAVELL

Armsdell,
July 15, 1945

Dear Lord Wavell,

1. After announcing the failure of the conference, you were good enough to ask for the support of all parties in ensuring a calm atmosphere. I do not propose to reiterate the Congress view about the failure. I expressed it sufficiently at the conference. But in fairness to you and to ourselves I must point out that co-operation inevitably depends on the removal of obstacles to it. Some of these obstacles are of a psychological nature with roots in the past relations between India and England. These can only gradually disappear with a change in those relations. But there are others of a more tangible kind which serve as constant irritants to our people and which affect our day to day activity. They are continually before us. In spite of this preoccupation, however, we did not think it desirable to raise this matter, except perhaps rather vaguely in the course of conversations with you, as we were anxious not to place any difficulties in your path when you were dealing with a delicate situation.

2. But now that one chapter has ended and our minds, as well as yours, are turned to future possibilities of finding a way out honourable to all concerned, and leading to the objective of Indian freedom, these obstacles to co-operation cannot be ignored. I am taking the liberty, therefore, of pointing them out to you in the hope that you will have early steps taken to have them removed.

3. The steps that I consider necessary and earnestly urge open you are:

(a) The bans on all Congress and allied organisations should removed at once. It has not been possible to convene the A.I.C.C. because of its being an illegal organisation.

(b) All detenus should be released without any condition being imposed upon them, whether the detention was imposed by the Central Government or the Provincial Governments.

(c) All restrictions on the movements of released detenus or prisoners should be removed.

(d) Cases of all prisoners convicted for political or like offences should be examined by a popular judicial tribunal and its verdict should be regarded as final by the Govt.

(e) Extra-legal restrictions on the freedom of the Press or on the movement or association of people should be removed so as to make the people feel that they are free to follow normal activities under democratic conditions.

(f) All pending sentences of hanging arising out of the disturbances of August 1942 should be commuted to life sentences.

(g) All pending arrests of "absconders" should be cancelled.

(h) All prisoners who have served full fourteen years should be unconditionally discharged.

(i) What has been said above about prisoners applies equally, and with even greater force, to properties, movable and immovable, and frozen or confiscated.

4. I have not endeavoured to argue out the justness of the foregoing requirements as I have no doubt that you will yourself appreciate the need for action along the lines indicated. If India is on the eve of having a *bona fide* national representative Executive, leading to independence after the defeat of Japan, then the necessity for this approach is self-proved and inevitable.

5. There is another matter to which I should like to refer. I need hardly say on behalf of the Congress that whatever, the result of your promised effort, Congress is and has always been against the Japanese aggression. Therefore, there will always be on the Congress a desire for the defeat of Japan in her designs upon China or any other aggression on her part. But the thought expressed in this paragraph will be incomplete if I did not inform you that, in the Congress estimation, the effort now being made on Indian soil will continue to be looked upon as a British and Allied effort, so long as there is not at the Centre a popular government assisted by provincial popular governments.

Yours sincerely,
A.K. Azad

Lord Wavell,
Viceregal Lodge, Simla

Document No. 15

TELEGRAM FROM MAULANA AZAD TO CLEMENT ATTLEE

27.07.1945

HEARTILY CONGRATULATIONS TO THE PEOPLE OF GREAT BRITAIN ON BEHALF OF THE PEOPLE OF INDIA ON THE RESULTS OF THE ELECTIONS, WHICH DEMONSTRATE THEIR ABANDONMENT OF OLD IDEAS AND ACCEPTANCE OF A NEW WORLD.

ABUL KALAM AZAD

Document No. 16

TELEGRAM FROM RAJAJI TO MAULANA AZAD

SEVAGRAM

Via Wardha (C.P.)

Sent 1.8.45

MAULANA ABUL KALAM AZAD
GULMARG
(KASHMIR)

PROPOSED DEMONSTRATIONS ALLAHABAD LIKELY DETERIORATE ATMOSPHERE AND STRENGTHEN UNIFRIENDLY ELEMENTS. I FEEL MATTER REQUIRES YOUR CONSIDERATION AND FURTHER DIRECTIONS TO LOCAL WORKERS.

RAJAGOPALACHARI

Document No. 17

LETTER FROM MAHATMA GANDHI TO MAULANA ABUL KALAM AZAD

Sevagram,
2nd August 1945

EXPRESS

Maulana Abul Kalam Azad
Gulmarg (Kashmir)

Your countenancing presentation to bereaved families in my opinion unwarranted in terms of non-violence and otherwise stop if you agree your reported approval and now inscription should be stopped.

Gandhi

Document No. 18

LETTER FROM GANDHIJI TO MAULANA ABUL KALAM AZAD

August 2, 1945

Dear Maulana Saheb,

I have your letter. I had asked Dr. Pattabhi.[1] I did not feel it was right to say anything when I had only seen the newspaper. Now that I have received the letter I shall be writing something. I have seen the telegram Rajaji has sent you. I agree with it. I saw something in the Press by way of a directive from you about providing for the relatives of those who died (during the struggle) in 1942 and afterwards. The financial help we are at present giving to such relatives for their maintenance and education is something different. In my opinion if we go by truth and non-violence we cannot give such assistance. How can we say that all of them died for the country, that they sacrificed themselves for the cause of Swaraj? I feel that under no circumstances can you do that. If I may advise you, I would ask you to withdraw the statement. I do not know whether there is still time for that. I am sending you a wire today.

The other thing concerns Begum Azad[2]. Dr. Khan Saheb mentioned the matter to me at Lahore. It pricked me. I am not aware of any public service rendered by Begum Azad. If what I believe is true, there should not be any public memorial in her name. Some persons came to me. I told them to do whatever they wanted. I did not have the courage to say anything more to them. But I can speak to you. I would advise you to issue a nice Press statement saying that since Begum Azad had not rendered any public service you would not like any public memorial in her name. If my advice does not appeal to you, you will please reject it. The love we hold for each other demands no less.

Yours,
M.K. Gandhi

---

1. Dr. B. Pattabhi Sitaramaiya.
2. Begum Zulaikha Khatun, wife of Maulana Azad.

Document No. 19

TELEGRAM FROM MAULANA ABUL KALAM AZAD TO MAHATMA GANDHI

Gulmarg,

5th August 1945

MAHATMA GANDHI,

INSCRIPTION IN MEMORY OF THOSE UNDERWENT VIOLENCE AND LOST LIVES THIS CANNOT STIR FEELINGS AGAINST NON-VIOLENCE STOP YOU KNOW I FULLY BELIEVE IN NON-VIOLENCE AS FAR AS NATIONAL STRUGGLE IS CONCERNED PLEASE READ INSCRIPTION ONCE AGAIN

ABUL KALAM AZAD

Document No. 20

LETTER FROM C. RAJAGOPALACHARI TO MAULANA AZAD

Sevagram,

8th August, 1945

Dear Maulana Saheb,

My attention has been brought to a very bad Leading article in the "Morning News" of Calcutta. I have at once written to the editor, a copy of which is enclosed. Somebody is at work deliberately inventing such stories. I understand that a similar story was attributed to Dr. Syed Mahmud. I have reasons now to think that also in probably a total invention from the same source.

C. Rajagopalachari

Maulana Abul Kalam Azad,
Gulmarg

Document No. 21

LETTER FROM C. RAJAGOPALACHARI TO MAULANA AZAD

Madra,

12.8.45

Dear Maulana Sahib,

I write this in pursuance of our conversation at Simla. Now that the points that compelled me to seek freedom of expression of my views through resignation of my membership of the Working Committee have ceased to be in controversy, I desire to serve the Congress duly enrolled as a member. The organisation not being in working order now, I write this to you to declare my acceptance of Article I and my membership may be recognised in the normal way by you as President. Needless to say my services are ever at your disposal if you deem them to be of any value.

Yours sincerely,
C. Rajagopalachari

Document No. 22

LETTER FROM MAHATMA GANDHI TO ABUL KALAM AZAD

Sevagram Wardha,
August 15, 1945

Dear Maulana Sahib,

On receipt of your letter today, I sent you the following wire: YOUR LETTER. I THINK IT SHOULD NOT BE PUBLISHED. WRITING FULLY.

I do not infer from your letter that you are writing about my 'Hindus'. Whatever, you have in your heart has not come in your writing. But do not worry about it. When we meet next we will talk over it if you so desire. Whatever you want to say about the communal problem should not be said without consulting the Working Committee. I am also of the opinion that it would be better to be quiet. The party can give its opinion after consultation with you. They have a right to do so, Besides it is their duty. I differ from your opinion. I can not say if I attach importance to the words 'Hindu' and Mussalman.' Whatever the Congress does is a different thing. At one time I do not like 'Hindu' and at another time I do not like 'Mussalman'. It means there cannot be either. All this needs pondering over. I do not feel the urge for doing anything early.

Yours
M.K. Gandhi

Document No. 23

STATEMENT OF MAULANA AZAD REGARDING THE COLLECTION OF BEGUM AZAD FUND

17.8.1945

I have learnt from Press reports that in various parts of the country efforts are being made to raise funds for a memorial to the late Begum Azad. I am deeply grateful to all friends who have undertaken this labour of love, and I consider it my duty to inform them of my own feelings and views regarding this matter. I believe that, in deciding to raise public memories to perpetuate anyone's memory, we must keep certain principles in view. Memorials should be raised only to persons who have rendered some distinct service to the country, or who occupy a special place in the estimation of the people on account of any personal distinction. Judged against this criterion the proposed memorial is hardly appropriate.

I have therefore, come to the conclusion that I must request all friends who have so far collected funds for this purpose to close these funds and transfer the amount collected to the Kamala Nehru Memorial Hospital, Allahabad. Once again I thank all these friends from the bottom of my heart.

Document No. 24

LETTER FROM MAULANA AZAD TO RAJAJI

Gulmarg (Kashmir),
August 19, 1945

My dear Rajaji,

I have just received your letter of the 12th August. I note with the greatest pleasure that you have become a member of the Congress anew. The time of separation was neither pleasant to you nor to us. It has, after all, come to an end and we are foregetting it for ever.

Yours sincerely,
A.K. Azad

Document No. 25

LETTER FROM MAULANA AZAD TO LORD WAVELL

Srinagar,
22.8.1945

Dear Lord Wavell,

I sent your Excellency the following telegram last night immediately after hearing over the radio the announcement that elections to the Central and Provincial Legislatures are going to be held as soon as possible:

> "Just heard radio announcement regarding elections to Central Legislatures before next Budget Session and early general elections to Provincial Legislatures. I cannot help registering my organisation's emphatic protest, for Congress is still under ban, political prisoners and detenus in prisons, many under severe handicaps, funds and properties confiscated, civil liberties drastically reduced under war-time Ordinances, and Defence of India Act and Rules still in operation, Cessation of hostilities in Europe was immediately followed by withdrawal of War-time measures and restoration of normal conditions in England for Electorate to express its will freely. It would be glaringly unjust to hold elections without first allowing Congress to function normally for sufficient time to organise elections."

In view of the urgency of the situation created by the announcement, I regret I was constrained to release the contents of the telegram to the Press.

It was on the 16th of July that I addressed you a letter about the restoration of normal conditions for the Congress to function, which included the lifting of the ban, release of the political prisoners and detenues and various other connected matters. The cessation of hostilities with Japan precipitated a situation.

Yours sincerely,
A.K. Azad

Lord Wavell,
Viceroy's House,
New Delhi

Document No. 26

LETTER FROM LORD WAVELL TO MAULANA ABUL KALAM AZAD

Vicroy's House,
New Delhi, 24 August 1945

Dear Maulana Sahib,

I regret that my reply to your letter of 15th July about the measures you recommend for the improvement of the political atmosphere has been delayed. I have now received your telegram of 21st August containing your views on the decision to hold general elections to the Central and Provincial Legislatures in the near future.

2. I deal below with the points raised in paragraph 3 of your letter.

(a) and (i) The bans on the A.I.C.C. and all orthodox Congress organisations have been, or will immediately be, removed. This will leave in force only those imposed by the Central Government on the Forward Bloc, the removal of which is being considered by the Home Department as a result of the Japanese surrender; by the Governments of the United Provinces, the Punjab, and Bihar on the Congress Socialist Party; and by certain Provincial Governments on local organisations which are fostering disorder.

As soon as a ban on any organisation is removed :

(i) Immovable property, of which possession only has been taken by the Government concerned, will be restored to its owners;

(ii) No legal process which has been completed in respect of movable property will be reversed and no money realised by the sale of such property will be returned; but any articles still in the possession of the Government concerned will be returned, provided that this decision will not extend to such movable property as it is illegal to possess and that no responsibility will be accepted for any loss or any deterioration in the property returned;

(iii) orders foreiting funds (including money's securities and credits) will not be upset, but funds frozen and not forfeited will be returned.

(b) and (c) The persons who have been detained without trial or on whose movements restrictions have been imposed have nearly all been in fact placed in preventive detention or have had their movements restricted because there were good grounds for believing that they were in communication with the enemy or that, judging from their past conduct, they were likely to engage in violent activities or terrorism. Now that Japan has surrendered their cases will be reviewed and some of them will no doubt be released as soon as the surrender is effective. But I fear there can be no question at present of indiscriminate releases. You will appreciate that some of the recent pronouncements by Congress leaders on the disturbances of 1942 are not reassuring to those responsible for maintaining law and order.

(d) I am not prepared to establish a special tribunal to examine the cases of all persons convicted for political offences. These persons have been properly tried and convicted by competent courts of justice.

(e) I am not aware of any restrictions on the freedom of the press or on the movement or association of people which can be described as "extralegal", and I am satisfied that in all Provinces unreasonable use is not being made of the legal powers that exist. These powers will not be used unfairly to hamper the activities of political parties during the elections.

(f) I have commuted to transportation for life the sentences of death passed in the Chimur-Ashti, Kulasekharapatnam, Fatwa and Jaunpur cases.

(g) I regret that I cannot pass a general order absolving absconders from liability to arrest. Many of these absconders have committed serious crimes.

(h) I will have the cases of all prisoners who have served more than 14 years examined.

In view of the surrender of Japan you will not, think, expect me to comment on paragraph 5 of your letter.

3. In your telegram of 21st August you suggest that normal conditions must be restored before elections can be held. After six years of war it seems to me impossible for India to return to normal order for some little time. Both Government and candidates have always in the past been strongly opposed to general elections except

in the winter months, so that the postponement of elections now would have meant a delay of one year. With the removal of the bans on orthodox Congress organisations and the accelerated release of persons still in detention I do not think that the Congress Party will be under any serious handicap. It is my aim to restore normal conditions as soon as I can. The Congress Party could assist me materially in doing so if they would refrain from public approbation of acts of violence.

Yours sincerely,
Wavell

Maulana Abul Kalam Azad,
Simla

Document No. 27

TELEGRAM FROM ABUL KALAM AZAD TO MAHATMA GANDHI

GULMARG,
25th AUGUST 1945

MAHATMA GANDHI

INSCRIPTION IN MEMORY OF THOSE UNDERWENT VIOLENCE AND LOST LIVES THIS CANNOT STIR FEELING AGAINST NON-VIOLENCE STOP YOU KNOW I FULLY BELIEVE IN NON-VIOLENCE AS FAR AS NATIONAL STRUGGLE IS CONCERNED PLEASE READ INSCRIPTION ONCE AGAIN.

ABUL KALAM AZAD

Document No. 28

LETTER FROM J.B. KRIPALANI TO MAULANA ABUL KALAM AZAD

Seth Mafatlal's Bungalow
Ganeshkind Road,
Poona-5

27th August 1945

My Dear Maulana Sahib,

I have already acknowledged your wire of the 24th from Bombay and informed you that what you wanted to be done was done. I hope you got my wire. I sent it to Srinagar.

As the ban on the A.I.C.C. has been removed in most of the Provinces and as you are anxious to have a meeting of that body at the earliest possible date, I would like to bring before you the question of the agenda for that meeting. You will agree that one of the important items on the agenda will be the activities of the Working Committee since the release of its members. In that connection the most important thing is the Simla Conference. The office in the past usually issued a bulletin after every meeting of the Working Committee recording its proceedings. Since our release we had two meetings of our committee, one in Bombay and another at Simla. And yet we have not issued our usual bulletin. It is by means of our bulletins that we keep the proceedings of the Working Committee before the A.I.C.C. and the public. This time we could not do it because of the embargo put by the Viceroy on the publication of your correspondence with him. This correspondence forms, from our point of view, a vital part of the proceedings of the Simla Conference. The public feel that they should have been taken into confidence immediately after the Conference broke up. They feel they have not enough material to form a correct judgment about the part we played at Simla. This is especially so when we are being constantly misrepresented by the Muslim League. I am sure the Viceroy immediately after the break-up of the Conference made his report to his Principals, the British Government. Our Principals are the people of India and it was unfair to prevent us from making a report to them specially when the other parties, the Government and the League, were not similarly prohibited.

But all this is past history. We could ignore the people. We cannot in the same way ignore the A.I.C.C. Even if we had such a desire, which I am sure we have not, we may not succeed. In my humble opinion, therefore, it is necessary that we issue a bulletin about the proceedings of the last two meetings of the Working Committee which will naturally contain all the relevant facts about the Simla Conference. This I feel must be done immediately. The bulletin may be marked 'Confidential' and may be distributed to the members of the A.I.C.C. at the time they meet. It is quite possible that the contents of such a bulletin may not remain quite confidential. But we have seen that even the proceedings of smaller executives, whether our own or governmental, remain confidential more in theory than in practice; and yet this fact does not prevent these bodies from transacting their necessary business.

There is another way of keeping the proceedings of the Simla Conference confidential and that is by calling a 'Secret Session' of the A.I.C.C. Even in that case some confidential white paper or bulletin about the Conference will have to be placed in the hands of the members to enable them to form a fair judgment of the part their representatives played at Simla and to discuss the matter, if they so desire.

I have kept my point of view before you. I would like to know what your own feelings in the matter are. I would also like to have your instructions about what is to be done, as early as possible.

I have sent you a telegram this day requesting you to wire to me your immediate programme.

I hope the change there has done some good to your health.

With best wishes and kind regards,

Yours sincerely,
J.B. Kripalani

Document No. 29

LETTER FROM PANDIT NEHRU TO MAULANA AZAD

Allahabad,
September 1, 1945

My dear Maulana,

I sent you a long telegram yesterday about the Punjab. I am now enclosing a copy of a letter which I am sending to Sardar Partap Singh, Secretary of the Punjab P.C.C.

Punjab affairs are fairly complicated as you know and there is a great deal that I could write about, but this will take a little time and I am afraid it might miss you in Srinagar. I might mention, however, that there is still some hope of some satisfactory solution being found there, for the present at least. I felt that the new group founded under Dr. Gopichand's leadership was acting in a rather narrow way. I tried to impress upon them not to do so.

The coming Assembly elections are naturally casting their shadow over Congress Work. In order to avoid this as possible I have suggested that election work should be separated, and should be put incharge of an election board to be appointed later in consultation with the all-India Board. This may make it easier to constitute a proper provincial executive.

One of the immediate issues is going to be the election to the Central Assembly, especially for the Sikh seat. As this election will precede others, some importance is attached to it. The question is whether a straightforward Congress Sikh candidate should be chosen, or whether someone who, though standing on the Congress ticket, has some affiliation with the Akalis. My own view favours the former course. It is probable that Master Tara Singh himself might stand for election. I think he should be opposed. As to who should oppose him it will be for your Central Parliamentary Board to consider. There is a strong element among the Sikhs who are wholly for the Congress and who are opposed to Akali politics. Among these specially are Sardar Amar Singh Jhabbal and his brother Sardar Sarmukh Singh

Jhabbal. Both of these brothers have long impressed me by their sincerity, but unfortunately the Akali group in the Congress executive does not approve of them. I shall speak about this to you more when we meet.

I am rather confused about the dates for the Working Committee Meeting. If the meeting is on the 12th I shall try to reach Bombay on the 11th and then go to Poona.

Yours affectionately,
Jawaharlal Nehru

Document No. 30

LETTER FROM MR. S.G. PATKAR TO MAULANA AZAD

Bombay, 15th September, 1945

Revered Maulana Sahib,

I, the undersigned, member of the Bombay Provincial Congress Committee, beg to submit the following appeal to the Working Committee of the Indian National Congress.

The Executive of the Bombay Provincial Congress Committee has taken the decision to remove me from the Committee and debar me from holding or contesting any elective position in the Congress for a period of three years from the 2nd September 1945.

My submission is that the decision of the B.P.C.C. is unjust and the method adopted in arriving at it is opposed to the democratic traditions of the Congress.

The proceedings were as follows :

On August 28, the General Secretary of the B.P.C.C. sent me a letter which contained the charges against me and which asked me to appear before the Executive on the 2nd September to submit my explanation in respect of the charges.

Accordingly, I appeared before the Executive and submitted a written statement. In the statement as also orally I contended that the letter made no concrete and specific charges against me beyond saying in a vague manner that I had acted against the spirit of the August Resolution. In the name of fairness I requested the Executive to frame their charges precisely and concretely.

At first the General Secretary of the B.P.C.C. refused to concede my request. But another member of the Executive, then still another, and finally the General Secretary himself came out with the following charges as an elucidation of the letter:

(1) That I helped the War effort;

(2) That I inculcated in the minds of the workers the spirit of opposing the August Resolution;

(3) That I was a member of the Communist Party of India.

Then Shri S.K. Patil made the offer that I should resign the membership of the Communist Party of India on doing which I would be absolved of all the charges.

I requested the Executive to give me reasonable time to enable me to give my replies to these charges and secondly in my own democratic right to give me an opportunity to appear before the Bombay Provincial Congress Committee. Both the requests were turned down, and the same day the decision of the Executive expelling me from the Bombay Provincial Congress Committee was communicated to me.

The Executive of the Bombay Provincial Congress Committee have done nothing to establish their charges against me. Nor did they bring forward any evidence in support of their charges. What I done during the last three years is already there in the statement I submitted to the Executive. I emphatically maintain that I cannot be charged with having violated the August Resolution either in spirit or letter. That I am a member of the Communist Party of India can certainly not be held as a breach of the August Resolution.

This is not all. The Executive Committee of the B.P.C.C. has not stopped at expelling me from the B.P.C.C. It has taken upon itself the authority of expelling me from the A.I.C.C. The General Secretary of the B.P.C.C. in his letter to me informs me that I cannot attend the forthcoming session of the A.I.C.C. In this connection, my submission is this that I am an A.I.C.C. member, not by virtue of being a B.P.C.C. member, but that I have been elected to the A.I.C.C. by the delegates to the Ramgarh Session of the Congress in a special meeting called for the purpose. The Executive Committee of the B.P.C.C. which also has some non-delegates as its members has not the authority to take any disciplinary action against any A.I.C.C. member. I can, threfore, be removed from the A.I.C.C. by the A.I.C.C. itself and in its absence by the President or the Working Committee of the Congress. The B.P.C.C. in expelling me from the A.I.C.C. and electing Mr. Bhavanjee Arjun Khimji to the A.I.C.C. in my place has gone beyond its powers and this violated the constitution of the Congress. I, therefore, submit that the decision of the B.P.C.C. is *ultra vires* and I appeal to the Working Committee to declare it null and void so that I may exercise my right to participate in the coming sittings of the A.I.C.C.

Yours fraternally,
S.G. Patkar

From :
S.G. Patkar,
C/O Bombay Girni Kamgar Union,
Dalvi Building,
Bombay-14

Document No. 31

LETTER FROM SEWANAND BALUKAKA TO MAULANA ABUL KALAM AZAD

Hinda Mata Mandir,
341, Sadashiv Peth,
Poona 2,

15th September, 1945

(A letter to Maulana Abul Kalam Azad, the President of the Indian National Congress, to be forwarded to the Sub-Committee, appointed to report about the problem of the Communist Party)

Respected Sir,

First a little bit of self-introduction. It is inevitable, as you, being comparatively a late-comer in Congress Politics, do not know me. Gandhiji knows very well from 1915 and our acquaintance continues up-to-date.

I am Sevak Sevanand Balukaka Kanitkar of Poona. I have been an active Congress Worker from 1906. I was the Secretary of the Poona City and District Congress Committees from 1928 to 1930.

I had the proud privilege of serving as the first head of the Satyagraha Committee of Poona in the glorious 1930 Satyagraha campaign. I was instrumental in sending hundreds of Satyagrahis to the different fronts in that memorable year, immortalised by the world famous Dandi March of Mahatma Gandhi. I have been into jail five times.

I took a very active part in the 1934 Bombay Session of the Congress, as a member of the All India Congress Committee. I moved the volunteer organization resolution; but could not get it passed as Gandhiji did not want it.

That year Gandhiji handed over the Congress into the hands of the Capitalist. He did this by doing away with the Khadi Clothes and by retaining the 4 annas condition for the Congress Voter. I asked him to do away with the 4 annas clause also, thus enabling even the poorest worker to get elected into any Congress Committee. He did not do it and in this way enabled the 'haves' to get themselves elected to all the Congress Committees by purchasing the votes of Congress Members by themselves paying their subscriptions through their paid agents. As you very well know they have actually done so. It is a bitter truth and was a great tragedy indeed.

I could not agree with this new power-politics policy and programme of the Congress, inaugurated by Gandhiji himself. So I resigned all my posts in the Executive Bodies of the Congress from top to bottom. I did this that I may be enabled to call a spade as spade, without being disloyal to the Congress creed. I did this as soon as the Congress Session was over.

I am still a 4 anna Congress member and mean to remain so, so long as the Congress creed remains as it is at present. I am still unofficially serving the Congress conscientiously to the best of my ability.

India is a nation of half-starved millions in rage. Its daily, average, per capita income is not more than, annas 2 at the most. While that of the Britisher is 45 annas and that of the American is 65 annas. So I have no faith in any top-heavy, expensive administration, *Swadeshi* or *Videshi*, foisted upon the nation by an interested, alien bureaucracy. I believe in the principle of self-determination and the most effective efficacy of truth and non-violent methods; and therefore I am convinced that the establishment of a parallel Government, based upon an ascending pyramid of self-reliant, self-sufficient, self-governing and self-protecting village republics is the only way of solving India's problem – political, economic, cultural as well as communal. I hate the very idea of Pakistan. I think it to be not only not practicable but I consider it to be terribly detrimental to the real interests of the Hindu and the Muslim Daridranarayan, the son of the soil. I am actively engaged in working out the scheme of Samarajya (commonwealth), in my own way. I have founded the Hinda Mata Congress, for that purpose; it proposes to achieve its object by establishing Hinda Mata Mandirs, in each and every village and by conducting all the nation-building activities on their behalf without having anything to do with the foreign bureaucracy.

As a member of the Indian National Congress, I consider it to be my sacred duty to draw your attention to certain important items in the policy, programme and constitution of the Congress. I hope you will kindly give your fullest possible attention to my appeal and do the needful in the matter. I will take the items one by one.

(1) I will first take the problem of the communist. Some people are talking of their expulsion from the Congress. Some Congress Committees are said to have passed resolutions to that effect. I am not a member of the Communist Party; still I think a great injustice is being done to that party when it is condemned for doing certain things for which it ought to be congratulated upon by the Congress.

(2) Why are the members of the party to be expelled? Because they condemned the movement which according to the utterances of several influential Congressmen was never started by the Congress at all. They are to be condemned because they expressed their strong disapproval of the movement of sabotage, which has been strongly condemned by Gandhiji and several prominent Congressmen as in their opinion it does not go hand in hand with the creed of the Congress, which wants to attain *swarajya* by all peaceful and legitimate means.

(3) If any party at all deserves condemnation at the hands of the Congress, it is the Congress Socialist Party. It deserves expulsion from the Congress because some of its prominent leaders started the movement of sobatage and took an active part in conducting it. Fortunately they failed in achieving their object and have now gone underground.

(4) Why not also pass a Resolution in strong condemnation of M/s Mashruwala and Kalelkar, who openly promulgated and encouraged some aspects of the sabotage movement in the *Harijan* columns? Mr. Mashruwala expressed repentance for his folly. But it does not in the least mitigate the offence, as all the mischief resulting from his stupid propaganda was already done. So it is highly necessary that there should be a permanent record of this condemnation in the Congress Books.

(5) Then there are certain Congress Committees who are said to have issued the detailed printed reports of their sabotage activities during the preceding year. I have personally read one such report, that published in the name of the Karnataka Provincial Congress Committee, the majority of whose members are known to be staunch followers of Gandhiji. Why not have an impartial tribunal for trying the case of these so called Gandhi followers? I can prove to the hilt their disloyalty to the Congress creed, policy and programme.

I can convince the tribunal of the utmost necessity of asking them to leave the Congress..

These gentlemen can carry on their activities like Bhagat Singhji and others manfully on their own responsibility. They should, on no account hid behind the name and prestige of Gandhiji and the Congress. It will prove to the public that they are not cowards and are ready to face the music of the consequences of their own policy and programme, be it good, bad or indifferent.

(6) The same can be said of certain other individuals. They are misleading the young generation, bubbling with patriotic fervour and uncontrollable enthusiasm. They are openly glorifying the sabotage movement of 1942. They are talking of repeating the same programme of sabotage activities of 1942 and of making it a thorough success.

The irony of the whole thing is that they are deceiving the public by calling themselves the followers of Gandhiji and the Congress. It is these persons who deserve immediate expulsion from the Congress, lock, stock and barrel.

(7) Now the Rashtra Seva Dal. This organisation is given recognition by the Congress Committees, Provincial and others, though it does not believe in non-violence, pure and simple. According to its own philosophy it has got certain exceptions in which it can have recourse to violence according to its own discretion. (Please read the marked portion on page 20 of Dala Prakash, Kiran 1st. It reads in English as follows: "....On such occasions it becomes necessary as a matter of course to act by considering certain duties as exceptions due to difficult conditions and by losening the bonds of non-violence. The soldier of the Rashtra Seva Dal may be an idealist of the first water. But the path of his ideal has to run through the grounds of practical politics. Therefore, he has to bow down, to certain exceptions even in the case of the ideal of non-violence in this world of practical politics...." My friend Mr. Shankerrao Deo will explain to you the remaining Marathi portion enclosed in the red lines.)

Every person and organisation has got every liberty to have its own philosophy. What I want to say is that they should not delude the public under false pretences by making it believe that they belong to the Congress. It is the duty of the Congress authorities to clear their own position and to free the public from this mischievous dillusion.

The fun of the whole thing is that the capitalist Councilwala Speculator is helping this organisation with the object that he should be able to exploit it in making its election campaign successful. And the sabotage leaders are taking great interest in it because they hope to make it the backbone and the spearhead of their next sabotage campaign. They have never made a secret of this intention of theirs. They have publicly declared it on several occasions.

(8) The Communist Party is to be condemned, because it helped the war-effort. So did the capitalist friends of Gandhiji, too. Why not condemn them also and ask them to leave the Congress? They helped the Government War effort actively by working their mills and factories by several shifts. They supported the Government War effort by working in several war committees, and by being members of several deputations for war purposes. Not only this but they have also prayed upon the poor public by their devil black marketing methods. They have made millions and millions by following a policy and programme, directly antagonistic to that of the Congress 1942 'Quit India' resolution.

So, if you are going to condemn and expell from the Congress the Communist you must also follow the same policy in the case of (a) The Congress Socialists (b) M/s Mashruwala, Kalelker and the other so called loyal followers of Gandhiji. (c) The different Provincial Congress Committees who indulged in sabotage activities, and advertised their doings publicly. (d) The Rashtra Seva Dal and (e) last but not the least the all powerful Sattawala Money-bags, the 'Geese that laid the golden eggs' for Gandhiji by their black markets and by wrecking the 1942 Congress programme and that have bribed Gandhiji into silence by filling the coffers of his various funds.

If you behave impartially in the case of all the various persons and parties mentioned above, then you can substantially prove your faith in truth and non-violence and revive the gradually declining faith of the thinking public in the *bona fides* of Gandhiji as well as that of the prominent Congress leaders, that are the powers that be in the present Congress hierarchy. You cannot deceive all people all times.

(9) The blind following of the Gullible, sentimental masses cannot be always counted upon by you. You will find this to your

> sorrow if you do not honestly follow the straight and narrow path of truth and non-violence but then it will be too late. It will be just like taking the horse to the fair after it is over. The terrible reaction which will result from your unwise policy will recoil on your own heads and the interests antagonistic to that of India, will be the only party which will be benefited thereby.

So on my bended knees I appeal to you not to condemn any person or any party and not even think of anybody being expelled from the Congress. You should let bygones be bygones, and by again reiterating your faith in the clearest possible terms in the truthful and non-violent nature of the Congress. You should invite all parties such as the Liberal Federation, the Hindu Mahasabha, the Ambedkarites, the Sikhs, and the Muslims, too, that have been unjustly forced into leaving the Congress to enter it again. At the same time you should not kowtow before any party to bring about a delusory communal unity. The only condition necessary should be their unadulterated loyalty to the Congress creed of peace and legitimacy, if they want to join the all-embracing Congress fold. Those enthusiasts, who want to achieve their object by following their own peculiar methods, such as Civil Disobedience, Sabotage, etc., should have their own independent organisations for that purpose. They should not commit the Congress to any particular fad of any party or person however great it or he may be. Then and then alone the Congress will cease to be dubbed as a party by its adversaries and will really deserve the name – the Indian National Congress.

The Congress revived in this manner will be the real, genuine constituent assembly of India. I do not believe in a constituent assembly, donated by an interested foreign nation, notoriously known as a nation of shop-keepers and historically known as perfidious Albeion.

This new Congress turned into a genuine constituent assembly should forge its own constitution and put it before the world, represented by the big five made up of Russia, China, France, America and England for their sanction. If this move be successful, well and good, if not then –.

There is the time-honoured method of Satyagraha, individually immortalised by Savitri, Pralhad, Markandaya, Dhruva, Vashishtha and others and which has been given a collective, national form by the Mahatma. The Mahatma then can independently carry out in the most non-violent manner, without anybody having recourse to any kind of sabotage, which does nothing but help the bureaucrat by playing into his hands, his old programme of making a Ganges of Indian blood flow from the Himalayas to the Cape. The nation, both the classes and the masses will be solidly behind him and will back him in every possible manner. This satyagraha will be the price which has to be paid for real independence. It will purify the nation and bring about a change of heart in those forces, both Swadeshi and Foreign, which are used by the foreigner to put down all the freedom activities of the Indian Nation. There will be a peaceful revolution in India and the world will be thrilled. It will receive a new lesson in the technique of non-violent and bloodless revolutions as well as a new culture and civilization which will bring about people and goodwill on earth and the Mahatma will deserve to be called a genuine 20th Century reincarnation of Gautam the Buddha and Jesus the Christ.

One last word and I finish. You must have already received the small pamphlet, entitled 'Sevanand to Gandhini' on behalf of the Satara Patriots. I am sure you have gone through it. If not I appeal to you to find time to read it and to do the needful.

If you have no objection I can see you personally to have an exchange of views about the subject-matter of this letter and about the Satara affair. You will please let me know the time and place of the meeting. In case I do not hear anything from you on Tuesday morning (18.9.45) I will send this letter to the press for publication.

With best respects,

I beg to remain,
Maulanaji,
Yours Ever in Comradeship,
Sevak Sewanand Balukaka Kanitkar.

Jai Hind !

Document No. 32

EXPRESS TELEGRAM FROM MAULANA AZAD TO LORD WAVELL

29, KOREGAON PARK
POONA 17.9.45

HIS EXCELLENCY VICEROY
NEW DELHI

I THANK YOU FOR YOUR LETTER OF TWENTY-FOURTH ULTIMO AND HOPE TO WRITE FULLY ABOUT VARIOUS MATTERS CONTAINED THEREIN SOON AFTER MEETING AICC STOP MEANWHILE I REGRET TO SAY THAT MANY CONGRESS PRISONERS AND DETENUS INCLUDING SEVERAL MEMBERS OF AICC AND ALSO PRESIDENT AND SECRETARY BENGAL PROVINCIAL COMMITTEE AND OTHER OFFICE-BEARERS OF CONGRESS COMMITTEES HAVE NOT YET BEEN RELEASED

ABUL KALAM AZAD

Document No. 33

LETTER FROM C. RAJAGOPALACHARI TO MAULANA AZAD

48, Bazalullah Road
Thyagarayanagar,
Madras

Poona, 19.9.45

Dear Maulana Sahib,

I have just seen the enclosed report in the press and wish to bring it to your notice and to state as follows:

I recognised my membership of the Congress in July 1942 as you are aware. On 12th September last, I wrote to you, asking you to permit me to rejoin the Congress and as President to accept my membership, seeing that at the time there was no membership enrolment and the Tamil Nadu P.C.C. was not functioning. You kindly accepted my request and wrote your letter to me of 19th September 1945. I communicate this facts to the secretary of the Taluka Committee of which, I had been a primary member. On that basis that Committee re-elected me to the P.C.C. The assumption that I had not been re-enrolled as a member of the Congress is therefore wrong. The election was duly conducted by the secretary of the Taluka Committee. The procedure laid down in Art. 23 was followed, *i.e.*, the vacancy was filled up in the same was as I had been originally chosen to that place, *viz.*, by election of the Taluka Congress Committee. Reference is made to Art. 7(C). Any objection based on Art. 7(C) is also untenable as after 1942, there was no enrolment of members whatsoever and neither I nor any one could possibly shown a three years membership at the time of my election 1945. No notice was issued to me by the Tamil Nadu Working Committee before they took this action of setting aside the election. The rule now proposed of filling up vacancies in committees by cooperation cannot affect what was done previously in my case. It was at first stated by the President of Tamil Nadu Congress Committee to a period interviewer that as the P.C.C. had not directed the Taluka Committee to fill up the vacancy. My election was invalid. The inherent right of a Taluka Committee to elect its delegate to the P.C.C. cannot be taken away by the default of the P.C.C. executive.

Yours sincerely,
C. Rajgopalachari

Document No. 34

MAIN PART OF THE ADDRESS OF MAULANA AZAD

11.09.1945,

To the A.I.C.C. Held in Bombay

All our minds are powerfully drawn towards a certain incident. Many incidents in our life come and pass on, but there are some which leave their imprint upon the robe of life which even time cannot erase. Just over three years ago, the A.I.C.C. meeting was held on exactly the same grounds. During these three years, a big story of India's national life has passed on. The story of these three years has two aspects : one of trials and tribulations and the other of the forces which have been created by these conditions. The power of nations springs from such hardship. An Arabic proverb says : Hardships have the same effect on life, as fire has on gold...

Document No. 35

LETTER FROM SARDAR PATEL TO MAULANA AZAD

Poona,
15 October, 1945

My dear Maulana Sahib,

The dates for the nomination of Central Assembly members are drawing near but I have not yet received the proposals from the provinces except from Kerala, which I have circulated amongst the members of the committee. But no reply has yet been received from them. I am afraid the procedure of circulation is cumbrous and lengthy. In many cases there will be more candidates than one for a constituency and there will be disputes. If I have to depend upon the procedure of circulation and wait for the replies from members I am afraid it would not be possible to dispose of the applications in time, nor is it possible to call a meeting where all members can attend in such a short time. Almost all the nomination dates are fixed in the last week of this month. There is therefore hardly any time for a meeting. Under the circumstances I will have no alternative but to give a decision according to my own light in case the replies are not received in time from the members of the committee. I have however kept a meeting here on the 21st and if some members will come, it will be helpful.

There is no change in the state of my health as yet, but I propose to go to Bombay on the 25th for a week for the work which you and the committee have entrusted to me and I hope to finish it largely during the course of that week.

I have heard nothing about the Central Assembly proposals from Bengal except Press reports saying that Sarat Babu is contesting the Central Assembly elections. I do not know what has happened there. Please ask the President of the BPCC to expedite the matter and to send me the proposals.

There is some dispute about Surma Valley and I had received a complaint from the Assam Provincial Congress Committee. I advised them to obtain your decision in the matter. I have not yet received the proposals from Assam also.

I had received a letter from Dr. Rajendra Prasad suggesting some sort of a settlement proposed by Dr. Shyama Prasad Mukerjee. He must have written to you also about it. I have opposed the proposals very strongly and written to Dr. Rajendra Prasad that the Congress cannot afford to enter into any settlement with the Hindu Mahasabha, which has no chance of winning any seat anywhere in the whole country. It would compromise our position without any compensating advantage. I do not know what advice you have given to him.

Both of us are anxious about your health. Please keep us informed about the state of your health and your activities and also take care of yourself.

Yours sincerely,
Vallabhbhai Patel

Maulana Abul Kalam Azad,
Calcutta

Document No. 36

LETTER FROM MAULANA AZAD TO SARDAR PATEL

Calcutta,
16 October, 1945

My dear Vallabhbhai,

I received your letter addressed to the Delhi address when I reached Lahore, but owing to pressure of work and indisposition I could not get time to look into the correspondence. The delay in reply could not be helped, which I hope you would not mind.

The day on which we had to meet in Bombay, I got ill, and diarrhoea, began all of a sudden. Dr. Gilder[1] and Dr. Mehta had examined me. Next day I went to Delhi, but the ailment continued and is still persisting. The treatment is going on.

Considering the present condition, the reorientation of the Congress Committee in Lahore is quite satisfactory, and it is hoped that work will go on smoothly till the formation of the new committees

I have sent a letter to Bapu in Hindustani, and have asked him to read out its contents to you also. I hope you have heard it, and would have formed an opinion in this respect.

So far as the candidates of the Punjab Central Assembly are concerned, the candidature of Mr. Brijlal Nehru[2] might be considered for the Lahore constituency. He is prepared to resign from Kashmir service.

Raizada Hansraj[3] was the member from Jullundur, probably he does not want to stand now. Kishori Lal Sethi[4] wants to stand from that constituency. We have, however, to wait for the recommendation of the Punjab Provincial Committee.

So far as the Muslim seats are concerned, the success of the Ahrars[5] and the Unionists[6] seems to be certain. They may get two or three seats on the Congress ticket also. The Ahrars are, however, in great need of help.

Yours sincerely,
A.K. Azad

1. Personal physician of Gandhi, Patel and other Congress leaders, later Health Minister in Bombay.
2. Former Auditor-General of Punjab and cousin of Jawaharlal Nehru; father of B.K. Nehru, Assam Governor.
3. Arya Samaj leader and Senior Congressman of Punjab.
4. Forest contractor of Kashmir; host of Gandhi and Nehru on their visits to Srinagar; member, Punjab Legislative Council after independence.
5. Members of militant Muslim political and religious organisation founded in 1928.
6. Members of Unionist Party of Punjab.

Document No. 37

LETTER FROM SARDAR PATEL TO MAULANA AZAD

Poona,
16, October, 1945

My dear Maulana Sahib,

The AICC by its Resolution No. VII has given directions for preparing an election manifesto to be placed before the next meeting of the AICC. But there is no possibility of the AICC meeting being held in the near future. I had therefore asked Jawaharlal to draft a manifesto for the Central Assembly elections. He has been good enough to prepare and has sent it to me. It has been corrected by Bapu and I have seen it also. I am herewith enclosing a copy of it[1] for your approval which may please be communicated to me by wire. As soon as your reply is received I will get it printed and circulate it amongst the various provinces.

Yours sincerely,
Vallabhbhai Patel

Maulana Abul Kalam Azad,
Calcutta

---

1. See document 70.

Document No. 38

LETTER FROM PT. JAWAHARLAL NEHRU TO ABUL KALAM AZAD

Allahabad,

16.10.45

My Dear Maulana,

I enclose a letter from Asaf Ali[1]. Yesterday I sent a telegram to you suggesting that you might issue a further statement about Indonesia. In Australia and elsewhere dock workers and seamen have refused to load arms and war material which was intended for use by the Dutch in Indonesia. It would be a good thing if our workers and seamen did likewise. The situation is critical and we should help in every way we can. I think meetings should also be held.

There is one other aspect of the question. It appears from the reports that Gurkha troops have been used against Indonesians. Would it not be desirable for an appeal to be made to the Nepal Government to prevent this improper use of their people?

Yours affectionately,
Jawaharlal

---

1. Not available.

Document No. 39

LETTER FROM MAULANA AZAD TO SARDAR PATEL

Calcutta,
19 October, 1945

My Dear Vallabhbhai,

The follwoing matters are to be taken into consideration in connection with the Central Assembly Election :

1. Mr. Maula Baksh has sent a letter to me from Karachi, in which he wants to draw the attention of the Board to the candidature of Sri Krishna Lulla, who has already sent his application to the local election board. It is, however, not known with what remarks his application would be forwarded by the local board to the Central Board. Maula Baksh has sent a copy of Lulla's application to me, which I am sending to you. What I have to say to you in this respect is that Maula Baksh is very keen on this gentlemen's nomination. He says that he was the right hand of his brother, and Nationalist Muslims of Sind would get ample support from him. He insists on his being adopted as a Congress candidate. If there be nothing against this man, we should not turn down the request of Maula Baksh, as we depend wholly on Maula Baksh in Sind, and we have to deal with him during the election and after it.
2. Sham Lal is the sitting member from Karnal-Ambala, but another man wants to contest this seat. I have directed him to put his case before the Punjab Board first. I do not know who has been recommended from the Punjab now. The man who wants to contest the seat of Sham Lal is said to have thrice opposed the Congress candidates and has never taken part in the Congress movement.
3. I had called here the representatives of Assam and Surma Valley. Now all their differences have come to an end, and it has been agreed upon that the work will be done by a

single joint board. The nominations of Surma Valley will, however, be made by the Bengal Board, because it is under Bengal's jurisdiction.

4. The Assam and Surma Valley Board is demanding funds for the Muslim seats. It is necessary that our arrangements be completed in this respect as soon as possible.

5. A suitable arrangement (for) Muslim seats has already been made in the Punjab. I am doing the same for Bengal also, but as no arrangement has yet been possible for the election fund, all the work is at a standstill and very valuable time is being lost. Please let me know without delay what you have done in this respect. I have not been able to do anything here, as the people have either gone out for the Puja, or they are busy in its celebration.

6. Dr. (P.C.) Ghosh and Kiran Sankar Roy were carrying on conversation with Mr. Sarat Chandra Bose about the election board while I was not here. I also continued it. Now a small board comprising Sarat Chandra Bose. Dr. Ghosh and Ashrafuddin Chowdhary has been formed. A bigger board will be necessary for the provincial elections.

I have not yet recouped my health. It is rest which I need most, but I am not getting it anywhere. Kindly let me know the present state of your health. I hope you would recover complete health through the treatment at Poona.

Yours sincerely,
A.K. Azad

Document No. 40

LETTER FROM MAULANA AZAD TO SARDAR PATEL

Calcutta,
21 October, 1945

My Dear Vallabhbhai,

Thanks for your letter of 15 October. I have already sent a registered letter to you, which might have reached by now.

1. I could not go to Peshawar owing to indisposition, but Bhanju Ram Gandhi[1] and Abdul Qayyum,[2] Secretary, PCC had come to Lahore and had a detailed talk with me. But the condition of the (NW) Frontier is unsatisfactory, and the Leaguers are putting in their full weight there. They are badly in need of money also. They should be helped immediately.
2. The Punjab and Bengal hold the key position in the present election. The result of the election will have far-reaching effects in future. The arrangement of the Punjab has been made to a certain extent and a board has been formed for the Muslim seats in Bengal. Both places need funds, specially Bengal, which will need the greatest amount.

I wanted to begin the election fund on my arrival here, but had to postpone it owing to Puja holidays. However, it will be begun in the first week of November, but the work should not stop on this account. A cheque of Rs. 20,000 was presented to me in Lahore. Though it was given to me, it was meant to be spent for the Punjab election. I wanted to send it to you, but now I have kept it back so that it might be utilised for urgent work here, if no other arrangement is made. Other arrangements would be possible in November only.

I hope Bengal will collect a good amount for election, but it will not be sufficient for the actual demands, and it would be necessary to get help from Bombay. The election campaign has to be carried on during this election in the Muslim majority provinces. We should spend the largest amount chiefly in these provinces.

3. Maula Bakhsh, Maulana Mohammad Sadiq and R.K. Sidhwa have written to me about Sind. A Muslim Nationalist Board has been formed there, and the conditions are hopeful but it is necessary that they should also get monetary help.
4. Rafi Ahmed Kidwai is doing the work in the U.P. who will write to you about his requirements in this connection. I do not know what has been done in Bihar by Rajendra Babu, but a fairly strong Nationalist Board has been formed there. It would achieve a good amount of success if it is duly helped.
5. Abdur Rahman is working for Kerala, I know nothing about the CP as yet. All my attention is centered on Muslim majority provinces.
6. Your reply to Rajendra Babu's letter is perfectly correct. All the workers of the U.P. and all the Congressmen of Bengal hold the same view. We should follow this line of action unflinchingly. I have taken full stock of every place – there is no chance for the Hindu Sabha in any province.

Yours sincerely,
A.K. Azad

---

1. Congress MLA (NWFP) 1936; joined Cabinet as Finance Minister, September, 1937; resigned in 1939; re-elected to Assembly, 1946.
2. Nationalist Muslim leader of NWFP; for some time Secretary of PCC and MLA; later defected to Muslim League.

Document No. 41

LETTER FROM DR. RAJENDRA PRASAD TO MAULANA AZAD

Camp Ranchi,
22nd October, 1945

My dear Maulana Saheb,

I have not heard any thing from you nor have I written anything to you since we parted at Bombay, I have in the meantime been trying to study the situation in my province. We have already sent our recommendation to the Congress Central Election Board for the Non-Muslim constituencies. The question of Muslims is still engaging our attention and if we find that we can set up suitable candidates with a fair chance of success we shall do so. In my province also a joint Board of Nationalist Muslims and the Congress Muslims has been formed. At the time I left Patna on the evening of the 19th last for a long tour of the province the Board was sitting to consider the question of candidates for the Central Assembly and we were awaiting its decisions before taking our own. I think it is desirable that you should make the position clear to the provincial committees in a communication addressed to them not necessarily by a public statement, on the following points:

1. The relation between the Nationalist Muslim Board and the provincial Congress Committees – whether the latter should nominate representatives on these Boards when invited to do so.
2. What should be our policy in regard to constituencies where Congressmen feel that candidates on purely Congress tickets can be returned should we allow any particular group such as the Momins or the Ulemas to set up candidates even for such seats?
3. I take it that in cases where the groups mentioned above have better chances than the Congress we should help them and should not set up any Congress candidates.

4. I take it also that in no case should there be a conflict between the congress and these groups.

All these will require prolonged discussion with regard to each constituency with groups and I should like to have clear guidance from you on these and other points which may strike.

I am out on a long tour of the province which ends about the end of November. Althrough my health is not good I consider the tour necessary and have undertaken it for strengthening the Congress organisation, collecting funds for sufferers and also helping the election campaign. Popular enthusiasm is great response to appeal for funds is splendid.

I hope your health is able to bear the strain which you are having. News about it is not reassuring but I pray that God may give you the strength.

I shall be obliged if Moulvi Ajmal Khan sends me a copy of the decisions arrived at by the Nationalist Muslims at Delhi.

With kind regards

Yours sincerely,
Rajendra Prasad

Document No. 42

LETTER FROM MAULANA AZAD TO SARDAR PATEL

Calcutta,
23 October, 1945

My dear Vallabhbhai,

Thanks for your last letter. I agree with the list of candidates which you have sent to me. Only about Dr. G.V. Deshmukh, who is standing from the Bombay city, I have to make an inquiry. Is he the same Deshmukh who was the sitting member, and who had issued malicious statements against Mahatma Gandhi? Moreover he has been breaking party discipline so often. If he is the same man, I think it will greatly damage Congress prestige to give him the Congress ticket. It has been repeatedly affirmed that only those persons will be allowed to contest the elections this time on behalf of the Congress who have taken part in the Congress movement and have proved their worth at the time of test. I do not know how we shall be able to keep up to our standard if we approve such a man ! I do not know what sacrifices he has made for the cause of the country.

It is quite possible that this is some other person. However, please let me know telegraphically about this matter.

I am receiving telegrams from the Punjab that the seat of Sham Lal, the sitting member, is being allotted to Thakurdas. The Central Board will have to intervene if the Punjab Board has made such a recommendation. Sham Lal and his family have always suffered for the Congress. It would be unjust to remove such a tried man. Thakurdas has always opposed Congress candidates, and always kept away from imprisonment. There could be no reason to give preference to such a man over Sham Lal. Thakurdas is the brother of Lala Gopichand Bhargava.[1] It should be brought home to Lala Gopichand that it is not proper for him for his own sake to get his brother's name adopted by the Congress. People have begun to say that he is using his influence unduly for his brother.

Yours sincerely,
A.K. Azad

---

1. Congress worker of Punjab since 1919; elected to Punjab Legislative Assembly in 1937 and again in 1946; Premier of Patiala and the East Punjab States Union (PEPSU), 1947-51.

Sardar Vallabhbhai Patel
Poona.

P.S.

In the first instance, the Board was formed in Calcutta very late and the other difficulty is that Sarat Babu is in Shillong, from where he will come here on the 28th or 29th. The result is that no names have yet been finally settled. It is hoped that it will be done on 28th or 29th instant. As no time will be left to send them to Poona, I shall accept them on behalf of the Central Board.

Azad

Document No. 43

LETTER FROM SARDAR PATEL TO MAULANA AZAD

Poona,

23 October, 1945

My Dear Maulana Sahib,

I have received your letter of the 16th inst. and I see that you are still in very poor health.

Bapu had your Hindustani letter to him read out to me as also his letter to you.

I wrote to you that Mr. Brijlal Nehru had withdrawn his proposal. Raizada Hansraj does want to stand from Jullundur and his proposal has been recommended by the Punjab Provincial Congress Committee unanimously. I have sent all the proposals of the Punjab to you, but as they were not quite complete and time was very short I had wired to Maulana Daud Ghaznavi to come here, and he is arriving here this evening. I have consulted all the members by circular. I have also consulted Dr. Pattabhi and Shri Shankerrao Deo[1] who attended the meeting. The Punjab proposals will be disposed of tomorrow after consulting the President of the Provincial Congress Committee. Diwan Chamanlal had also come here the day before yesterday. Tentative decisions have already been taken by the committee.

I am going to Bombay tomorrow and I had to dispose of the proposals so far received before leaving this place as there was pressure from all provinces for early disposal. Forty-three nominations have already been sanctioned and announced except from Bengal and Punjab and two seats from Madras. All others have been disposed of. The largest number of complaints were from Madras, but I had called the president of the Tamil Nadu PCC and the secretaries of the Andhra and Kerala PCCs, and after consultation with them the Board unanimously disposed of ten seats. The remaining two will be disposed of on receiving further information which they will wire to me after necessary enquiries.

As for Bengal you and Prafulla (P.C. Ghosh) may dispose of the matter after consulting the local leaders and inform me of the action taken by you.

In the Punjab there are two Sikh seats of which one will be contested by Sardar Kapoor Singh on our behalf. He is a strong candidate and we will win. But the other seat for which Sardar Sardul Singh Caveeshar was proposed will be contested by Sardar Sampuran Singh on behalf of the Akalis[2] and we are sure to lose. The other two candidates proposed are stronger than Sardar Sardul Singh but even then they will not probably succeed. It is now proposed that Sardar Sant Singh[3] who has subsequently applied and is a much stronger candidate and is sure to win should be set up for this constituency. This question will be decided tomorrow after consulting Maulana Ghaznavi.

Re. the three Hindu seats. About the one from Ambala Division in which Babu Thakurdas Bhargava and Lala Sham Lal are rival candidates, we will select Babu Thakurdas who is strongly recommended by Mr. Asaf Ali and with which recommendation the Board has agreed. The other seat will be contested by Raizada Hansraj. The third is a difficult one and Maulana Ghaznavi had wired to me to persuade Diwan Chamanlal to stand. In case he declines I should keep the question open. Both Chamanlal and Maulana Ghaznavi will be consulted tomorrow and I will communicate the decision to you. After this consultation they will have to go back straight to Lahore tomorrow because the nomination date is very near.

This will dispose of all the Central Assembly selections, except Bengal.

I am going to Bombay for a week tomorrow afternoon and will write to you after my return from Bombay.

Yours sincerely,
Vallabhbhai Patel

Maulana Abul Kalam Azad,
Calcutta

---

1. Congress leader from Maharashtra; joined non-cooperation movement in 1920, member, AICC and Working Committee of Congress. Chairman, Reception Committee, Faizpur Congress 1936; member of CA from Bombay.
2. Sikh devotees of cult founded by Guru Govind Singh (died 1708); now members of a politico-religious party of Sikhs.
3. Member of Central Assembly from Punjab with pro-Congress leanings.

Document No. 44

TELEGRAM OF MAULANA AZAD TO SARDAR PATEL

Calcutta,
25 October, 1945

Sardar Vallabhbhai Patel,
Congress House,
Bombay

WIRED YESTERDAY POONA ABOUT B. DAS (CUTTACK) APPEAL AGAINST REJECTION HIS NAME. PLEASE RECONSIDER. HE IS QUITE FIT FOR WORK.

ABULKALAM AZAD

Document No. 45

LETTER FROM SARDAR PATEL TO MAULANA AZAD

26 October, 1945

Dear Maulana Sahib,

I have received your letter of the 21st instant today. Your telegram about Mr. B. Das of Orissa was received late last night and I have replied as under:

> COMMITTEE REJECTED B. DAS FOR GOOD REASONS. CALLED FOR SUBSTITUTE WHOSE NAME ALREADY SANCTIONED AND COMMUNICATED. IMPOSSIBLE CHANCE NOW.

Mr. (H.K.) Mahtab[1] had discussed this matter with me while he was at Poona and he himself was opposed to his nomination. Apart from his being physically not quite fit for being sent to the Central Assembly, there were other reasons also. Subsequently, no doubt, his name was recommended as no other candidate probably was available within the short period of the notice for application. But the Committee at Poona considered the whole question carefully and wired to Shri Mahtab to send fresh proposals which were eventually received and sanctioned by the committee. The proposal was communicated to Shri Mahtab and also to the candidate. It was therefore impossible at this stage to make any changes as suggested in your telegram. Mr. B. Das was also informed about the decision of the Committee.

About the Frontier I am arranging for help immediately.

In the Punjab, the Akalis are on the Warpath. They have started violence in public meetings. The two candidates selected by us are fairly strong and the Akalis have lost their temper. Maulana Daud Ghaznavi and Diwan Chamanlal had both come to me at Poona and we have fixed up the nominations in consultation with them. They have accompanied me to Bombay and both of them left yesterday for Lahore. Dr. Gopichand is here at my instance for securing financial assistance from here for the Punjab. He will be returning back after a couple of days.

The Bengal Central Assembly elections are a little later than in other provinces. I have not yet received the proposals from there. The provincial elections will, I believe, take place in February or March. But no programme has yet been announced. Sarat Babu is still at Kurseong. I believe he has written to you about his talks with the Muslim groups. But unfortunately you are not in a fit state of health. Unless you, Prafulla Babu, Sarat and the Muslim leaders meet and decide as to the whole plan of action in Bengal we cannot see our way clearly. You may also be able to ascertain roughly what should be the amount required for fighting the elections in Bengal. There should be no difficulty in raising the money required from Bengal, but even if there is any difficulty we can meet with it if we have some idea about your requirements there.

It is good that you have kept the cheque for Rs. 20,000 presented to you in the Punjab for the work to be done there at present.

Your telegram about selecting Shri Krishna Lulla from Sind for the Central Assembly at the suggestion of Maula Baksh was also received very late after the decision of the committee was communicated to the Sind Provincial Congress Committee. I have wired to Jairamdas Doulatram[1] if it is possible to readjust the matter in the light of your recommendation. But I fear they would not be able to do so at this late stage.

The Hindu Mahasabha has been creating unnecessary trouble by putting up candidates everywhere. In Bombay they have at the last moment put up two worthless candidates, the principal one of whom was defeated badly in a municipal by-election last year. But for this normal opposition there would have been no contest in Bombay. But this will involve us expenditure for nothing.

In Gujarat so far as the Central Assembly is concerned, our candidates go unopposed, So in Mahakoshal. But in Maharashtra, the Hindu Mahasabha has been opposing us. Probably they will do so except in Gujarat and Mahakoshal.

I have also received a letter from Rajen Babu asking for financial help, and I am arranging to meet this demand immediately.

Arrangements are also being made for Assam. Prabhu Dayal came here yesterday as I had written to him from Poona. I have seen his requirements and there will be no difficulty about that province at all. I have advised him to contest all the Muslim seats. They had at first decided not to contest a large number of Muslim seats for fear of financial difficulties. But I have advised them as above and they have accepted my advice.

At present I am concentrating on my work here and later on when I am able to leave the clinic at Poona, I will go to some other places where it would be necessary for me to go for finishing my work.

In Delhi also I hear from Mr. Asaf Ali that the Hindu Mahasabha is putting up a candidate against him. I do not know whether this kind of opposition is intended to coerce us to enter into a settlement with them or whether there is any other object behind it.

What does the Hindu Mahasabha propose to do in Bengal about the Central Assembly seats?

Yours sincerely,
Vallabhbhai Patel

---

1. Member, AICC, 1917-41; MLC (Bombay), 1927-29; General Secretary, AICC, 1931-34: Member, Congress Working Committee; Member, CA 1946; Bihar Governor, 1947; Later Union Food Minister and Governor, Assam.

Document No. 46

TELEGRAM FROM MAULANA AZAD TO SARDAR PATEL

Calcutta,
October 26, 1945

Sardar Vallabhbhai Patel,
Congress House,
Bombay

THAKURDAS BHARGAV'S NOMINATION OBJECTIONABLE. HAS ALWAYS OPPOSED CONGRESS CANDIDATE. NEVER PARTICIPATED MOVEMENT. NEVERTHELESS GOPI CHAND – BROTHER. I CANNOT AGREE SUCH NOMINATION.

ABUL KALAM AZAD

Document No. 47

TELEGRAM FROM MAULANA AZAD'S TO SARDAR PATEL

Calcutta,

28 October, 1945

THE SITTING MEMBER FROM AMBALA-HISSAR IS A TRIED AND TRUSTED MAN OF THE CONGRESS. HE HIMSELF, ALONG WITH HIS SON AND DAUGHTER-IN-LAW, HAS CONSTANTLY BEEN GOING TO JAIL, AND HAS NEVER STAYED BACK IN ANY MOVEMENT. THAKURDAS HAS DONE NO SUCH SERVICE. HE OPPOSED CONGRESS CANDIDATES THRICE, AND ALWAYS KEPT HIMSELF ALOOF FROM IMPRISONMENT. NOTHING CAN BE SAID IN HIS FAVOUR FROM THE CONGRESS POINT OF VIEW EXCEPT THAT HE IS THE BROTHER OF LALA GOPICHAND. PERHAPS THESE FACTS WERE NOT BROUGHT TO YOUR NOTICE. KINDLY REVISE THE SELECTION OF THAKURDAS AND ANNOUNCE THE NAME OF SHAMLAL. SHAMLAL HAS APPEALED AGAINST THIS SELECTION. I AM AWAITING YOUR REPLY.

Document No. 48

TELEGRAM FROM SARDAR PATEL'S TO MAULANA AZAD

Bombay,

29 October 1945

YOUR MESSAGE RECEIVED LATE LAST NIGHT, REGRET IMPOSSIBLE REVISE DECISION. FOUR MEMBERS OF CENTRAL BOARD OUT OF SEVEN VOTED FOR THAKURDAS. TWO ACQUIESCED IN THE DECISION. COMMITTEE CONSIDERED QUESTION THOROUGHLY. AWAITED YOUR REPLY TILL 22ND EVENTUALLY DECIDED AND DECISION WAS ANNOUNCED 24TH.

I HAVE NO AUTHORITY UPSET COMMITTEE'S DECISION NOW AS THAT WOULD TANTAMOUNT TO VOTE OF CENSURE AGAINST COMMITTEE AND WOULD RESULT IN SERIOUS REPERCUSSIONS CENTRAL BOARD AS WELL AS LOCAL.

REGARDING YOUR TELEGRAM ABOUT SIND CANDIDATE JAIRAMDAS WIRES – MAN RECOMMENDED BY YOU COMES FOURTH IN ORDER OF MERIT OUT OF FOUR CANDIDATES AND LIKELY TO LOSE SEAT IF ACCEPTED.

Document No. 49

LETTER FROM LORD WAVELL TO MAULANA AZAD

Viceroy's House, New Delhi,
29 October, 1945

Dear Maulana Sahib,

1. I have received your letter of 10th October, and note your general observations about the need for goodwill at the present time. The enclosed extracts from newspaper reports of speeches and statements made by Congress leaders before, during and after the Simla Conference, seem to me to indicate that the Government of India are not wholly responsible for the absence of good-will of which you complain.

2. My replies to your more detailed points are as follows:

(a) and (i). The only bans now subsisting, so far as I know, are those against the Forward Bloc throughout India; the Congress Socialist Party in the United Provinces, the Punjab and Bihar, and in Nagpur in the Central Provinces; the Hindustan Red Army in Nagpur and Umrao in the Central Provinces; the Rashtriya Sewak Dal in the Satara District of Bombay; and the Shanti Senas in Assam. The Government of India do not wish to maintain these bans longer than is necessary, but I am surprised that you believe that the Congress Socialist Party "adheres to the policies of the Congress." The attitude of the Congress Socialist Party has been summarized as follows in a statement generally attributed to its General Secretary and not so far as I am aware repudiated by any member of the Party:

"My own interpretation of the Congress position – not Gandhiji's – is clear and definite ... We are justified ... to fight Britain with arms. If this does not accord with Gandhiji's principles, that is not my fault."

"In every firka, taluqa, and thana and in every considerable factory and workshop and other industrial centre we must

> have a band of militants, mentally and materially equipped for the next rising."

I was not aware that the Congress Party had officially approved methods and objects of this kind which is what your letter seems to imply.

The subsisting bans do not in my opinion "operate as a serious handicap in respect to elections," since there is nothing to prevent any individual standing for election, and the Congress, which you describe as "the parent organisation," is not banned.

The immovable property of individuals cannot be takenover by Government under the Criminal Law Amendment Act, nor (unless it is requisitioned or acquired for public purposes) under the Defence of India Act or Rules. I am therefore not clear as to the cases of immovable property that you have in mind. The decision not to reverse legal processes by which movable property and funds have been finally forfeited was taken on practical grounds, and I am unable to reconsider it.

(b) and (c). The persons still in detention for reasons in any way connected with politics numbered about 1,100 on 1st October 1945. All of them are persons whose past conduct show that they are likely to engage in violent activities or terrorism. I agree that there was delay in reviewing the restriction orders in the Delhi Province, but I understand that nearly all of them have now been cancelled, and that generally the number of restriction orders has been very greatly reduced.

(d) I regret I cannot change my view about the establishment of a Special Tribunal.

(e) There is still a shortage of newsprint, of which all Parties alike complain. I satisfied myself on a recent complaint from the President of the Hindu Mahasabha that the supplies available are distributed fairly, and there is nothing more to be done until supplies improve.

(f) No comment is needed.

(g) For the reasons already given, I am unable to pass a general order absolving all absconders from liability to arrest.

(h) The cases to which you refer are still under consideration.

3. Prospective candidates who desire the removal of a disqualification should if they wish to stand for the Central Legislative Assembly apply to Government of India in the Legislative Department

for the orders of the Governor-General-in-Council; of if they wish to stand for a Provincial Legislature to the Governor concerned.

The case of Mr. Biswanath Das was considered by the Governor-General-in-Council who decided not to remove his disqualification for election to the Central Assembly. He had been found guilty of a corrupt practice which disqualified him absolutely for election to the Orissa Assembly for six years; the offence was not technical; and the Governor-General-in-Council saw no reason why in the circumstances his disqualification should be removed.

4. I am sure you will appreciate that it would be quite impossible to allow special priority in respect of supplies and movement to members of one political party. The Government of India are in correspondence with Provincial Governments about the special supply of petrol to all Parties for election purposes, and every possible effort will be made, having regard to the continuing shortage of petrol, to make adequate supplies available. I am informed that there should be no serious difficulty about paper. There is no priority system for travel by train, and the pressure on air transport for urgent official purposes is so heavy that special priority for persons engaged in the elections is impossible.

5. I note your remarks about the electoral rolls. All Provincial Governments are doing their best to amend them as well as possible in the time available.

Yours sincerely,
Wavell

Maulana Azad,
Swaraj Bhawan,
Allahabad

Document No. 50

LETTER FROM PT. JAWAHARLAL NEHRU TO MAULANA AZAD

Allahabad,
October 31, 1945

My dear Maulana,

I am receiving demands from all over the country for election tours. I do not know what to do and where to go. I should like to go to the Frontier Province and to Bengal specially. Of course my own province has a prior claim on me. I have so far not even visited great cities such as Benares, Cawnpore, Agra and Meerut, or many of the afflicted areas. Much of my time is being taken up by the I.N.A. work and the National Planning Committee.

There is a matter which distresses me. I find, almost everywhere that I go, small cliques controlling Congress committees and preventing enthusiastic workers from coming in or doing any work. There is a very big gulf between these committees and the public. The public is enthusiastic for the Congress, but often the committees are not popular. They are stale and old and often consist of people who have never worked.

From such reports as I get the situation in the Punjab is very unsatisfactory and the same old groups which have done so little in the past are again in control and new people are kept out.

Also reports in the papers of some nominations for the elections are surprising, specially from the Punjab, Sind and Bengal. I know that you are in a better position to judge and I should not interfere in any way. I do not propose to interfere but I wanted to tell you how distressed I was about all this. If I go on an election tour it becomes very difficult for me to say anything in support of a candidate who seems to be undesirable. Questions are put to me and I do not know how to answer them, because my own previous statements are put before me.

I received your telegram last night about Rafi being in-charge of the U.P. and Delhi. I do not quite know what this means but Rafi is on his way to Calcutta and you will no doubt explain it to him.

Yours affectionately,
Jawaharlal

Document No. 51

LETTER FROM MAHATMA GANDHI TO MAULANA ABUL KALAM AZAD

November 1, 1945

Bhai Saheb,

I have your letter. What more shall I say about your health? The sooner you go somewhere for rest the better it will be for the country. You have sent three names for the Working Committee. It will be better if in this matter you consult the present members and then announce the names. I have an impression that the Congress will have to meet some time soon. In that case will it not be better if the vacancies are filled by fresh elections? But if they have to be filled now, I think the three names that you have sent are all right. However, the members will be the best judges.

Yours,
M.K. Gandhi

Maulana Abul Kalam Azad,
19-A, Ballygunje, Circular Road,
Calcutta

Document No. 52

LETTER FROM SARDAR PATEL TO MAULANA AZAD

Poona,
6 November, 1945

My dear Maulana Sahib,

On my return from Bombay on the 3rd evening, I learned from Bapu that you propose to call a meeting of the Working Committee at Calcutta on or about 16 December. A subsequent letter from Prafulla Babu indicates your intention to keep it in the last week of December. As it is, the middle of December will in itself be late, but the end of December will be too late. I expected that you will keep it in the first week of December when Bapu reaches there. You know we have promised a manifesto to the AICC for the provincial elections. The elections in some provinces will be in early January and we must be ready with the manifesto. It all depends upon your health and if you are going out for a change then it would not be possible to keep the meeting earlier.

About the Central Election Board, an early meeting is very necessary. We have to decide our attitude regarding the proposals for nominations for the provincial elections. In Sind they have already made some tentative proposals and I expect they will be submitting them to us shortly. These proposals will be of a very controversial nature and it would not be possible to dispose of them by correspondence. I, therefore, propose to call a meeting here on Friday, 16 November, and settle the question of policy to be adopted in the matter of these elections. As far as the Central Assembly was concerned, we had decided that the provinces should send their proposals with their report and the final selection was to be made by us. In several provinces the old committees are out of touch with the present-day atmosphere and they do not enjoy the confidence of the real workers of the Congress. If the selection is to be left to the provinces I am afraid there will be serious trouble and it will be difficult to impose discipline. If the final selections are to be made by the Board, we must send our instructions to the provinces as soon possible and we must also decide about the procedure to be adopted by our Board in this behalf. Regarding the Central Assembly elections, we had very little time and therefore some of the complaints were received even after the nomination date was over. So far as the provinces are concerned such difficulty is likely to arise if we delay the decision regarding the procedure to be adopted in the matter.

I know that you would not be able to leave Calcutta or perhaps you will be going soon to some place for a change. Hence, your coming to any place for the meeting is impossible. But if the rest of the members meet and discuss amongst themselves all the different points involved in the matter of selection of provincial nomianations, it would be easy for the Board to make a report for your advice and opinion, and then we can come to some final decision. We may not take any decision in the Board till your approval is obtained, but the informal talks would be very helpful. If you suggest any other procedure I would unhesitatingly adopt it, but at present no other way occurs to me for the solution of this difficulty. I shall expect your reply whether the meeting should be called on the 16th or not by wire so that I can communicate with other members of the Board in time.

I have arranged to send a cheque of Rs. 25,000 from Bombay which you must have received by this time. Yesterday I received Prafulla Babu's letter giving me an idea of your joint deliberations about the estimate which I had asked for. His letter indicates a huge sum. Indeed, for one province alone it is staggering, but I shall try to do my best and see that our cause does not suffer on that account.

Today Sarat Babu is coming in the afternoon and I propose to send this letter with him.

I am expecting to hear from you where and when you are going for a change and when you expect to return, so that in case of emergency I may possibly communicate with you through a messenger.

I hope you are taking care of your health. I am leaving this place for Bombay on the 19th. Bapu also goes on that day.

Yours sincerely
Vallabhbhai Patel

Maulana Abul Kalam Azad,
Calcutta

Document No. 53

LETTER FROM MAULANA AZAD TO SARDAR PATEL

Calcutta,

6.11.1945

My dear Vallabhbhai,

I have just received a cheque for rupees 20,000 from Bombay. Please send me another cheque for rupees 25,000 as soon as you receive this letter. I am leaving for Bindhachal tommorrow. Please send the cheque at the Bindhachal address.

Yours sincerely,
A.K. Azad

Sardar Vallabhbhai Patel,

Poona

Document No. 54

LETTER FROM MAULANA AZAD TO LORD WAVELL

Swaraj Bhawan, Allahabad,
7 November, 1945

Dear Lord Wavell,

I have to thank your Excellency for your letter of October 27th, 1945. I appreciate the frankness with which you have expressed yourself on the question of relations between Congress and the Government, and I propose to place before you my views and feelings with equal frankness. I trust you will take my observations and remarks in the spirit in which they are offered.

I would like at the very outset to draw your attention to the fact that we were all released on the 15th of June this year, after incarceration of about three years. The condition of detention is such that it is naturally bound to weigh upon one's mind, and in our case our irritation and anger was enhanced by the reports of events and incidents outside. Some of us suffered in addition from deep personal loss and sorrow. All these factors, it was inevitable, should induce a state of mind that would not but express itself the moment we were released. Emotions that were long and forcibly suppressed, sought and found echo in the feelings of our countrymen from whom we were (had) so long been separated.

Bitter feelings were almost inevitable in such circumstances, and yet, I believe, you will admit that I made a strong effort to forget the past and shape our action in the light of changed circumstances, and the Working Committee was fully with me in these efforts. You know that I along with my colleagues accepted the invitation to the Simla Conference in the hope that this marked a new phase in the history of Indo-British relations. The Congress worked for an improvement of the atmosphere, and went to great lengths for an amicable settlement.

You are aware that the Congress has always taken a very strong stand on the question of the veto of the Governor-General, and this was one of the Chief reasons for the rejection of the Cripps offer.

The offer made by you did not satisfy the Congress demand on this point, but even this was not allowed to stand in the way of Congress' attempt at peaceful settlement. You will, I believe, yourself admit that there was neither rancour nor recrimination in the Congress attitude; and if the Simla Conference failed, this was not on account of the Congress, but in spite of it.

In spite of the failure of the Conference we believed that the contacts established between the Congress and the Government had largely allayed past bitterness, and marked the beginning of a new chapter of confidence and goodwill.

As a result of these contacts, the people naturally hoped that there would be an immediate change in the Government's attitude to Congress, the ban on the A.I.C.C. and other Congress organisations would be lifted and all political prisoners released, in order to create a new and better atmosphere. It was for this reason that, before I left Simla, I wrote to you on the 16th July, and urged that in order to maintain improvement in the atmosphere, you should take steps for immediate release of political prisoners and detenus. I am confident that if this had been done, the changed atmosphere would have led the people to forget past conflict and bitterness.

Soon after this the results of the general elections in Britain were published, and the Labour Party came into power. Some of my colleagues were inclined to believe that Labour's accession to power was of little import to us. But I was of a different opinion, and felt that we should not judge the Labour Cabinet without a trial. Accordingly I welcomed the new Cabinet and sent my congratulations to some of its members.

Events since then have not justified my hipes. No change in the Indian policy was felt, and the administrative pattern shows little signs of change. Even at the time you announced the General Elections in your broadcast of August last, the ban on the A.I.C.C. was not removed, and my repeated representations for a general release of all political prisoners was unheeded.

All these facts, *viz.*, the failure of the Simla Conference, and the circumstances in which it failed, the absence of any marked change in the Indian policy even after the change of government in England, and above all the continuation of the old attitude of distrust to the Congress organisation could not but influence the attitude of political workers.

The Labour Party have said again and again that they want the chance of solving the Indian problem peacefully. They have now got the chance; and I am prepared to do everything possible for the creation and maintenance of a peaceful atmosphere. But my hands must be strengthened if I am to be able to carry my countrymen with me. It is obviously impossible for me to do so unless the Government also prove by their action that they want to create the atmosphere for such a peaceful change. There must be a wiping of the slate, and we must start afresh. The continued incarceration of even one political prisoner offends against such an atmosphere and acts both as reminder of the past and an irritant in the present.

There are two other matters to which I would like to refer. The first is in respect of your reference in paragraph 2(a) and (c) to the ban on the Congress Socialist Party. You have quoted an extract from a document alleged to have been written by the General Secretary of the Congress Socialist Party, and expressed your surprise at my insistence on lifting the ban on it. You yourself say that the passage is "attributed" to the General Secretary of the Congress Socialist Party. In other words, even the Government have no definite proof on the point. It is obviously impossible for the Congress to take any decision in the absence of fuller and clearer information. On the other hand, the declared creed and policy of the Congress is well-known. No member can go against them, and if anyone does, the Congress has power of taking disciplinary action against him. You will remember that the Congress has not hesitated to take such action against some of its most prominent members, when circumstances warranted such action. The Congress Socialist Party was formed within the aegis of the Congress, and has never repudiated the Congress creed and policy. If the passage quoted by you is really an expression of its policy, this would be in direct conflict with Congress, and the Congress would not hesitate to take necessary steps against it. This cannot, however, be done so long as the C.S. Party is under a ban and its leaders in jail. Once the ban is removed and the leaders released, the party would either conform to Congress creed and policy or deviate from it. If it did deviate, the Congress would itself take necessary action against the party.

I come finally to the extracts you have enclosed of speeches and statements by different Congress leaders. The first two are mine, and I will deal with them first. Soon after my release, I was interviewed by a representative of *The Statesman*, Calcutta. He drew my attention to the repeated Government declaration since 1942, that there could be no understanding with the Congress, so long as the Congress thought in terms of a mass movement during the period of war, and asked what our attitude would be, if the Simla Conference failed. My reply was that there should not be a mass movement in the war period. Here, there was a clear indication of our desire not to embarrass the Government during the continuation of the war, and I fail to understand how this can in any way justify the absence of goodwill on the part of the Government.

The second extract is very much in the same spirit. This was no speech or statement of mine, and I could not at first recollect it. On looking up the *Amrita Bazar Patrika* of 27th July I found that some persons had come to see me, and it is their report of the interview. Asked about Congress attitude towards violence and non-violence, I made it clear that the Congress would depend only on non-violent mass movement for achieving its ends, but in any case, there should not in my opinion, be any such movement during the period of the war. If, however, the aim of independence cannot be realised through negotiation and settlement, Congress must face the task and take steps to strengthen the masses for any future contingency after the war. Surely nobody can expect Indians to declare that whatever be the situation in the future, they will never initiate or join a struggle for achieving their freedom.

The quotations from the speeches of my colleagues only confirm what I have said earlier in my letter. It is patent that the last three years are full of the record of conflict and discord. In an atmosphere of "forgive and forget" these memories would soon fade; but in its absence it is elementary human nature that there should be a revival of bitter memories.

I want to impress upon you that I have not approached this question in a spirit of diplomacy or political bargaining. I have expressed what is in my heart and my reading of the times makes me feel that a peaceful and honourable settlement of the Indian question is possible and all my efforts shall be directed to that end.

There is one small point to which also I desire to draw your attention. All my letters are still being censored, causing unnecessary delay in all my correspondence. Letters are delivered to me three or four days after they are due and there are marks of tampering in many of them. This is annoying at any time and more so during an election campaign. I could not attend the meeting of the Central Congress Parliamentary Board and had to decide many questions through correspondence. You can easily understand the inconvenience and interference by delay of three or four days on either side.

In conclusion, I must apologise for the length of the letter and the intrusion upon your valuable time, but I trust you will not mind this in view of the importance of clarity in discussing the attitude and policy of the Congress.

Yours sincerely,
A.K. Azad

Document No. 55

LETTER FROM SARDAR PATEL TO MAULANA AZAD

Poona,
11.11.1945

My dear Maulana Saheb,

I have received your letter of the 6th instant and I am issuing instructions for sending you another amount of Rs. 25,000 from Bombay as desired by you in your letter. Evidently you have not received the letter I sent to you with Sarat Babu,[1] probably because you had left Calcutta before he reached there.

Yours sincerely,
Vallabhbhai Patel

Maulana Abul Kalam Azad,
Bindhachal (U.P.)

---

1. Sarat Chandra Bose, elder brother of Netaji Subhash Chandra Bose and a member of Interim Government in 1946, headed by Pandit Jawaharlal Nehru.

Document No. 56

TELEGRAM OF NEHRU AND PATEL TO MAULANA AZAD

POONA,

12 NOVEMBER, 1945

MAULANA ABUL KALAM AZAD
BINDHACHAL

IN VIEW URGENCY PREPARATION ELECTION MANIFESTO CONSIDERATION OTHER IMPORTANT PROBLEMS SUGGEST WORKING COMMITTEE MEETING CALCUTTA FIRST WEEK DECEMBER.

VALLABHBHAI
JAWAHARLAL

Document No. 57

TELEGRAM FROM MAULANA AZAD TO SARDAR PATEL

BINDHACHAL,
12 NOVEMBER, 1945

SARDAR VALLABHBHAI PATEL,
POONA

YOUR LETTER CALLING BOARD'S MEETING UNNECESSARY FOR DECIDING PROCEDURE. WE DECIDED AT POONA THAT CENTRAL BOARD WILL APPROVE PROVINCIAL CANDIDATES AND CONSULT PROVINCIAL REPRESENTATIONS. INTEND CALLING WORKING COMMITTEE AND BOARD'S MEETING BETWEEN TENTH AND FIFTEENTH DECEMBER. PLEASE WIRE.

ABULKALAMAZAD

Document No. 58

TELEGRAM OF SARDAR PATEL TO MAULANA AZAD

POONA,
12 NOVEMBER, 1945

MAULANA ABUL KALAM AZAD,
BINDHACHAL

YOUR WIRE. CERTAIN PROVINCIAL PROPOSALS SPECIALLY SIND UNITED PROVINCES ASSAM BIHAR REQUIRE IMMEDIATE SANCTION. PLEASE AUTHORISE OR SUGGEST ALTERNATIVE METHOD SPEEDY DISPOSAL. WE WOULD PREFER WORKING COMMITTEE (MEETING) EARLY DECEMBER AS ALREADY TELEGRAPHED.

VALLABHBHAI

Document No. 59

LETTER FROM SARDAR PATEL TO MAULANA AZAD

Poona,

13 November 1945

My dear Maulana Sahib,

I have received your letter of the 7th inst. along with the bills for Rs. 7,370/3/- today. I am issuing instructions for doing the needful in the matter.

We have sent you a telegram for fixing the meeting of the Working Committee early in the first week of December. In the meanwhile I received from you a reply to my letter which was sent to you through Sarat Babu. We considered the whole matter again and we came to the conclusion that an early meeting would be advisable. Another telegram was therefore sent to you. I am expecting your reply today. Jawaharlal has returned to Bombay.

This morning I got a telegram from Sarat Babu reading:

> MAULVI WALUR RAHMAN CANDIDATE PRESIDENCY-*CUM*-BURDWAN AND MAULVI MOHUDDIN KHAN CANDIDATE RAJSHAHI DIVISION MOHAMEDAN CONSTITUENCIES CENTRAL ASSEMBLY INFORMED ME AND PRESIDENT BPCC ON TENTH THAT THEY WOULD STAND ON CONGRESS TICKET AND NO OTHER TICKET. PLEASE APPROVE AND MAKE NECESSARY ANNOUNCEMENT.
>
> SARAT BOSE

It would be a good thing if we can get two members on the Congress ticket for the Central Assembly. So far we have got none.

Yesterday I had sent you a circular letter about the proposals of the Sind Provincial Congress Committee for the Provincial Assembly. Since then I have received some complaints about some of the proposals which will also be circulated today.

You must have seen from the Press that Mr. (Abdullah) Haroon,[1] the League candidate, is being opposed by Mr. Rashid Ali,[2] who has been expelled from the league. Haroon is a rich man and the contest is going to be very severe. Rashid Ali needs financial help. Mr. Vazirani recommends him and he has also written to me promising his support to us after the election. He needs a big amount.

Hope you are doing well and the change is doing you good.

Yours sincerely,
Vallabhbhai Patel

Maulana Abul Kalam Azad,
Bindhachal

1. Leading merchant of Karachi and Congressman, 1920-28; parted company with Congress to advocate separation of Sind from Bombay Presidency and later supported Muslim League.
2. Muslim Leaguer and man of letters and journalist, office-bearer of the Moslem, Jumait, Karachi.

Document No. 60

LETTER FROM MAULANA AZAD TO SARDAR PATEL

Bindhachal,
Mirzapore, U.P.,
13.11.1945

My dear Vallabhbhai,

I have come to Bindhachal since 8 November (1945). I could not get your letter in Calcutta because Mr. Sarat Chandra Bose reached there on the 9th. It was sent to me here through a messenger, thus there was a delay of three days in the transmission. I have sent to you my opinion by an express telegram[1] immediately on receipt of the letter.

You must remember that we had declared in Poona and Bombay that the names of the candidates for the provincial Assemblies should also come to the Centre for approval, as this cannot be left to the present Committee. We had also decided that the Provincial representatives might also be called, if need be, for the consultation of the Central Board before the final approval. It, therefore, seems to be unnecessary to call a meeting of the board to lay down the Procedure. The Procedure has already been settled and the Provinces are also not unaware of it. The only thing to be done now is that a date be fixed up to which time the recommendations of the Provinces might reach the centre.

I agree with you that the meeting of Congress Working Committee and the Board be called as soon as possible. I will fix it between 10 and 15 of December. It will be held in Calcutta as Bapu[2] is going there.

Mathura Babu[3] had come here with a letter from Rajendra Babu.[4] Please send him a sum of rupees 25,000 for the election fund. He is pressing hard for it.

Yours sincerely,
A.K. Azad

Sardar Vallabhbhai Patel,
Poona

---

1. Maulana Azad had sent a telegram to Vallabhbhai Patel on 13.11.45 in reply of his letter of 6th November, 1945 informing him about his Poona talk and suggesting him of unnecessary of calling a meeting of Central Election Board.
2. Mahatma Gandhi.
3. Mathura Das.
4. Dr. Rajendra Prasad.

Document No. 61

LETTER FROM MAULANA AZAD TO ACHARYA KRIPALANI

Bindhachal,
15.11.45

My dear Kripalani,

I hope you are doing quite well now.

We had decided at Poona that 30th November would be the last date for the enrolment of the Primary Members of the Congress. At the same time we had decided that if some places would really feel the need for extension of time, the President would do so. Now the United Provinces, and specially Bengal, are pressing for some more time for the enrolment. Under the circumstances, I consider that the time may be extended for two weeks more, *i.e.*, the last date should be 15th December. Please inform U.P. and Bengal accordingly.

Yours sincerely,
A.K. Azad

Acharya J.B. Kripalani,
General Secretary A.I.C.C.,
Swaraj Bhavan,
Allahabad

Document No. 62

TELEGRAM FROM SARDAR PATEL TO MAULANA AZAD

POONA,
15 NOVEMBER, 1945

MAULANA ABUL KALAM AZAD
BINDHACHAL

THIS MONTH OTHER MEMBERS ENGAGED ASSEMBLY ELECTIONS. DIFFICULT LEAVING THEIR PROVINCES. GANDHIJI'S PROGRAMME FIXED FOR SEVAGRAM TILL END MONTH. SUGGEST YOUR DISPOSING SIND PROPOSALS.

VALLABHBHAI

Document No. 63

TELEGRAM FROM MAULANA AZAD TO SARDAR PATEL

BINDHACHAL,
15 NOVEMBER, 1945

SARDAR VALLABHBHAI PATEL,
POONA

AS SIND ELECTIONS VERY NEAR HOLDING BOARD'S MEETING 24TH AND WORKING (COMMITTEE) 26TH ALLAHABAD, CALCUTTA CLIMATE VERY DETRIMENTAL TO MY HEALTH. IT WOULD GREATLY HELP IF WITHOUT RETURNING CALCUTTA I COULD DO IT. PLEASE CONSULT BAPU AND WIRE.

ABULKALAMAZAD

Document No. 64

LETTER FROM SARDAR PATEL TO MAULANA AZAD

Poona,
15 November, 1945

My dear Maulana Sahib,

I have just received your telegram suggesting our meeting on the 24 at Allahabad. The members of our (Parliamentary) Board are all engaged in the Central Assembly elections in their respective provinces and they are not in a position to break their engagements or to leave their province. I have got letters from both Rajen Babu and Pantji in which the former says that his programme is fixed till 5 December for his tour in the province and the latter also till the end of this month. Shankarrao (Deo) also has his programme fixed till the end of this month in Maharashtra and Nagpur. Dr. Pattabhi also is busy with his election campaign as the Madras city election is on 1 December. It is therefore not possible for them to leave their provinces.

Bapu has fixed his programme for Sevagram where several meetings are kept during the last week of this month. Under the circumstances our meeting is out of the question in the course of this month. But we must dispose of the Sind proposals which are urgent. I had wired to Dr. Choithram Gidwani to come to Bombay as soon as possible after the 19th with all the proposals including the applications rejected by them as also the complaints and protests. It is my intention to send all materials with a report to you at Bindhachal.

Whether Dr. Choithram will come or not I do not know. I have wired to him yesterday but there is no reply. I would therefore suggest that you may dispose of the Sind proposals yourself in the manner you like, so that there may be no difficulty if we meet a little later.

The proposals for the Scheduled Castes from the U.P. have been approved by me in anticipation of sanction as their date of nomination was on the 10th. Most of these seats have been contested and others have filed their nominations.

The Assam Scheduled Castes' proposals have also been received and they are also such as would raise no controversy and the other members of the committee are hardly interested in it.

The Bihar Scheduled Castes' proposals are also expected tomorrow. They may also be disposed of in accordance with the recommendation of the province as they are hardly such as would interest any other member outside the province.

The proposals for the general constituencies from other provinces will probably come in the first week of December or even later. So, if the Sind proposals are disposed of there would be no urgency for our meeting. I have therefore sent the following telegram to you in consultation with Bapu:

> THIS MONTH OTHER MEMBER ENGAGED ASSEMBLY ELECTIONS DIFFICULTY LEAVING THEIR PROVINCES. GANDHIJI'S PROGRAMME FIXED FOR SEVAGRAM TILL END MONTH, SUGGEST YOUR DISPOSING SIND PROPOSALS.

Yours sincerely,
Vallabhbhai Patel

Maulana Abul Kalam Azad,
Bindhachal

Document No. 65

LETTER FROM SARDAR PATEL TO MAULANA AZAD

24 November, 1945

My Dear Maulana Sahib,

The Punjab nominations have at last forced your hands and you had to advance the date of the Working Committee Meeting. It will interfere with your required rest. The Punjab nominations will probably be very controversial, but I have not yet received the proposals. They are busy with the Central Assembly Elections, and they will probably be free today. There are two constituencies about which decision will have to be taken immediately: the one is about the university and the other about commerce. These elections are likely to take place earlier. For the university seat, I hear that if Sjt. Bhim Sen Sachar is asked to stand, we may get it uncontested, or even if there is a contest, there would be no difficulty about winning it. The present incumbent is Sir Manohar Lal. There is one complication in this affair. Sjt. Bhim Sen's father-in-law has declared his candidature for this seat. He is a title-holder, but is prepared to give up his title and accept the Congress ticket, if given. How far we can trust such people is a question. If Sjt. Bhim Sen[1] is asked to stand, he will withdraw. This is what I have heard but I have got no proposals as yet. About the other seat also, I have not received any proposals. If there is any proposal received here, I will communicate to you by telegram for your advice, if there is urgency. The remaining proposals will be disposed of when we meet at Calcutta.

I hope your stay at Bindhachal has improved your health.

The situation in Calcutta in the meanwhile has greatly deteriorated. There has been firing several times and unfortunately the students have shown great indiscipline. It compromises our position as a national organisation. The local leaders have not been able to control the crowds. This kind of indiscipline is spreading and we must take strong action to improve the situation in future.

Hope you are doing well.

Yours sincerely,
Vallabhbhai

Maulana Abul Kalam Azad
Bindhachal

---

1. Bhim Sen Sachar

Document No. 66

LETTER FROM MAULANA AZAD TO DR. RAJENDRA PRASAD

Camp Bindhachal,

25.11.45

My dear Rajendra Babu,

Your letter of 20th November, with the enclosed letter, has been received by me. As the C.W.C. is being held in Calcutta on the 6th December, it would be better to postpone this matter till then. We will decide this matter in the meeting there.

The Central Board is meeting in Calcutta on the 4th December. It is hoped that you will reach there by that time.

Yours sincerely,
A.K. Azad

Dr. Rajendra Prasad,
Sadakat Ashram,
Patna

Document No. 67

LETTER FROM PANDIT JAWAHARLAL NEHRU TO MAULANA AZAD

Allahabad,
November 27, 1945

My dear Maulana,

I have just come back from touring the Meerut division. I feel tired and my throat is bad. But I have to go again immediately to Lucknow for a meeting of the P.C.C. Council. I wanted very much to pay you a visit but I do not see how I can do it. On my return from Lucknow I shall spend a day and half here and then go to Delhi for a day. When I was in Delhi last I received a letter from Sir Claude Auchinleck, the Commander-in-Chief, saying that he would be glad to meet me and have a talk. He mentioned several dates. In my reply I chose one of these dates December 1st. So I presume I shall have to go to Delhi for this purpose. I hope to return by the 2nd afternoon.

I understand that you are going by air from Allahabad to Calcutta and that you are likely to come to Allahabad on the 2nd afternoon or evening. If so, I shall of course meet you here. I propose to go to Calcutta on the 4th December.

My brief visit to the Punjab has not produced very favourable impressions on my mind. Probably we shall win the two Sikh seats. But so far everything is vague about the Provincial elections. Maulvi Daud Ghaznavi is a good man but the party spirit in the Punjab and the extremely narrow outlook of most people there prevents solid work being done. I have no doubt that the ground is favourable. I hope still that the Punjab Congress will shake itself up and do something.

In the Meerut division and elsewhere I have found an extraordinary favourable response from the Muslim masses. Whether we win these seats or not on this occasion, I have no doubt in my mind that we can win quite a number of Muslim seats in the Provincial elections in the U.P. specially in the rural areas. I was surprised to find how popular the Congress was among Muslim peasantry. In fact the Jamiat did not go far with them, it was the Congress that counted. In the cities, the Jamiat influenced people more. On the whole, however, it was obvious that the Congress counted. It is pretty clear that we have long neglected the Muslim masses. The fault lies with us not with them.

Prafulla Babu has telegraphed to me to postpone my visit to Calcutta. So this is not fixed yet. I still want to go there, especially to Midnapore, if Prafulla Babu agrees. He wants me to go on a longer visit later. But no one knows what will happen later.

The Indonesian struggle is becoming more intense and critical and I feel that we ought to give it greater prominence. It would be a good thing if there were meetings etc. But the most dramatic thing would be for our dock workers and seamen to refuse to load war material for Java, as the Australians did.

Yours,
Jawaharlal

Document No. 68

LETTER FROM MAULANA AZAD TO RAJAJI

Camp Bindhachal
27.11.45

My dear Rajaji,

I hope to be excused for the delay in replying your letters. I wished to get all the necessary details of the matter.

Please let me know whether at the time of your election as a Delegate and member of the P.C.C. from the Trichingoda Taluka Committee :

1. There was or was not the Register of Members there?
2. The members were called and admitted in the meeting according to the register or not?
3. The meeting was held with the knowledge and permission of the provincial Committee or not?

Moreover, I would like to have a copy of the proceeding of the meeting, and a copy of the correspondence, if any, with the Provincial Congress Committee.

The matter of Malayan Indians was already under my consideration, and I have done the needful.

Yours sincerely,
A.K. Azad

Sri C. Rajagopalachari,
Thyagarayanagar,
Bazlullah Road,
Madras

Document No. 69

LETTER FROM P.S. TO MAULANA AZAD TO RAJAJI

Allahabad

December 10, 1945

My dear Rajaji,

I have received your letters, and have heard the deputation fully. I have consulted Bapu also. Taking all the circumstances into consideration, I am doing what I can in this respect. Please rest assured.

Yours sincerely,
A.K. Azad
(Signed by M. Azmal Khan as Maulana Sahib is in Singapore from where he will return in the evening.)

Sri Rajgopalachariar,
Bazlullah Road,
Thyagarayanagar,
Madras

Document No. 70

THE CONGRESS MANIFESTO FOR CENTRAL AND THE PROVINCIAL ELECTIONS WITH MAULANA AZAD AS PRESIDENT

11.12.1945

"The All India Congress Committee at its meeting held in Bombay in September last resolved that a manifesto containing the policy and programme of the Congress for the information of the public and the guidance of the Congress candidates in the forthcoming general elections be prepared by the Working Committee and placed before the A.I.C.C. for consideration and adoption. Further it authorised the Working Committee to issue an earlier manifesto for the Central Assembly elections. Accordingly this later election manifesto has already been issued to the public. The Working Committee regret that owing to the nearness of the general elections in the provinces it is not feasible now to hold a meeting of the A.I.C.C. in the near future to consider the fuller manifesto, as contemplated by the A.I.C.C. They have, therefore, themselves prepared this manifesto and issue it for the information of the public and guidance of Congress candidates."

The following is the full text of the Manifesto:

"For sixty years the National Congress has laboured for the freedom of India. During this long span of years its history has been the history of the Indian people, straining at the leash that has held them in bondage, ever trying to unloose themselves from it. From small beginnings it has progressively grown and spread in this vast country, carrying the message of freedom to the masses of our people in the towns as well as the remotest villages. From these masses it has gained power and strength and developed into a mighty orgaisation, the living and vibrant symbol of India's will to freedom and independence. From generation to generation it has dedicated itself to this sacred cause, and in its name and under its banner innumerable countrymen and countrywomen of ours have laid down their lives and undergone suffering in order to redeem the pledge they had taken. By service and sacrifice it has enshrined itself in the hearts of our people; by its refusal to submit to any dishonour to our nation it has built up a powerful movement of resistance to foreign rule."

Stronger than ever

The carrer of the Congress has been one of both constructive effort for the good of the people and of unceasing struggle to gain freedom. In this struggle it has faced numerous crises and come repeatedly into direct conflict with the armed might of a great empire. Following peaceful methods, it has not only survived these conflicts but has gained new strength from them. After the recent three years of an unprecedented mass upheaval and its cruel and ruthless suppression, the Congress has risen stronger than ever and become more loved by the people by whom it has stood through storm and stress.

Equal Rights for all

The Congress has stood for equal rights and opportunities for every citizen of India, man or woman. It has stood for the unity of all communities and religious groups and for tolerance and goodwill between them. It has stood for full opportunities for the people as a whole to grow and develop according to their own wishes and genius; it has also stood for the freedom of each group and territorial area within the nation to develop its own life and culture within the larger framework, and it has stated that for this purpose such territorial areas or provinces should be constituted, as far as possible, on a linguistic and cultural basis. It has stood for the rights of all those who suffer from social tyranny and injustice and for the removal of them of all barriers to equality.

The Congress has envisaged a free democratic state with the fundamental rights and liberties of all its citizens guaranteed in the constitution. This constitution in its view should be a federal one with autonomy for its constituent units, and its legislative organs elected under universal adult franchise. The federation of India must be a willing union of its various parts. In order to give the maximum of freedom to the constituent units there may be a minimum list of common and essential federal subjects which will apply to all units, and a further optional list of common subjects which may be accepted by such units as desire to do so.

Constitutional Rights

The constitution shall provide for fundamental rights, among them the following:

(1) Every citizen of India has the right of free expression of opinion, the right of free association and combination, and the right to assemble peacefully and without arms, for a purpose not opposed to law or morality.

(2) Every citizen shall enjoy freedom of conscience and the right freely to profess and practise his religion, subject to public order and morality.

(3) The culture, language and script of the minorities and of the different linguistic areas shall be protected.

(4) All citizens are equal before the law, irrespective of religion, caste, creed or sex.

(5) No disability attaches to any citizen by reason of his or her religion, caste, creed or sex, in regard to public employment, office of power or honour, and in the exercise of any trade or calling.

(6) All citizens have equal rights in regard to wells, tanks, roads, schools and places of public resort, maintained out of state or local funds, or dedicated by private persons for the use of the general public.

(7) Every citizen has the right to keep and bear arms, in accordance with regulations and reservations made in that behalf.

(8) No person shall be deprived of his liberty, nor shall his dwelling or property be entered, sequestered, or confiscated, save in accordance with law.

(9) The state shall observe neutrality in regard to all religions.

(10) The franchise shall be on the basis of universal adult suffrage.

(11) The state shall provide for free and compulsory basic education.

(12) Every citizen is free to move throughout India and to stay and settle in any part thereof, to follow any trade or calling, and to be treated equally with regard to legal prosecution or protection in all parts of India.

The State shall further provide all necessary safeguards for the protection and the development of the backward or suppressed elements in the population, so that they might make rapid progress and take a full and equal part in national life. In particular, the state will help in the development of the people of the tribal areas in a manner most suited to their genius, and in the education and social and economic progress of the scheduled classes.

Numerous Problems

A hundred and fifty years and more of foreign rule have arrested the growth of the country and produced numerous vital problems that demand immediate solution. Intensive exploitation of the country and the people during this period has reduced the masses to the depths of misery and starvation. The country has not only been politically kept under subjection and humiliated, but has also suffered economic, social, cultural and spiritual degradation. During the years of war this process of exploitation by irresponsible authority in utter disregard of Indian interests and views, and an incompetence in administration reached a new height leading to terrible famine and widespread misery. There is no way to solving any of these urgent problems except through freedom and independence. The content of political freedom must be both economic and social.

Removing Poverty

The most vital and urgent of India's problems is how to remove the curse of poverty and raise the standard of the masses. It is to the well-being and progress of these masses that the Congress has directed its special attention and its constructive activities. It is by their well-being and advancement that it has judged every proposal and every change, and it has declared that anything that comes in the way of the good of the masses of our country must be removed. Industry and agriculture, the social services and public utilities must be encouraged, modernised and rapidly extended in order to add to the wealth of the country and give it the capacity for self-growth without dependence on others. But all this must be done with the primary object of benefiting the masses of our people and raising their economic, cultural and spiritual level, removing unemployment, and adding to the dignity of the individual. For this purpose it will be necessary to plan and co-ordinate social advance in all its many fields, to prevent the concentration of wealth and power in the hands of individuals and groups, to prevent vested interests inimical to society from growing, and to have social control of the mineral resources, means of transport and the principal methods of production and distribution in land, industry and in other departments of national activity, so that free

India may develop into a co-operative commonwealth. The state must therefore own or control key and basic industries and services, mineral resources, railways, waterways, shipping and other means of public transport. Currency and exchange, banking and insurance, must be regulated in the national interest.

A Rural Problem

Though poverty is widespread in India, it is essentially a rural problem caused chiefly by overpressure on land and lack of other wealth-producing occupations. India, under British rule, has been progressively ruralised, many of her avenues of work and employment closed, and a vast mass of the population thrown on the land, which has undergone continuous fragmentation, till a very large number of holdings have become uneconomic. It is essential, therefore, that the problem of the land should be dealt with in all its aspects. Agriculture has to be improved on scientific lines and industry has to be developed rapidly in its various forms – large scale, medium and small so as not only to produce wealth but also to absorb people from the land. In particular, cottage industries have to be encouraged, both as whole-time and part-time occupations. It is essential that in planning and the development of industry, while maximum wealth production for the community should be aimed at, it should be borne in mind that this is not done at the cost of creating fresh unemployment. Planning must lead to maximum employment, indeed to the employment of every able-bodied person. Landless labourers should have opportunities of work offered to them and be absorbed in agriculture or industry.

Reform of Land System

The reform of the land system, which is so urgently needed in India, involves the removal of intermediaries between the peasant and the state. The rights of such intermediaries should therefore be acquired on payment of equitable compensation. While individualist farming or peasant proprietorship should continue, progressive agriculture as well as the creation of new social values and incentives require some system of co-operative farming suited to Indian conditions. Any such change can, however, be made only with the goodwill and agreement of the peasantry concerned. It is desirable, therefore, that experimental co-operative farms should be organised with State help in various parts of India. There should also be large State farms for demonstrative and experimental purposes.

Developmment of Land

In the development of land and industry there has to be a proper integration and balance between rural and urban economy. In the past, rural economy has suffered, and the town and city have prospered at the cost of village. This has to be righted and an attempt made to equalise, so far as possible, the standars of life of town dwellers and villagers. Industry should not be concentrated in particular provinces, so as to give a balanced economy to each province, and it should be decentralized, as far as this is possible without sacrifice of efficiency.

Both the development of land and of industry, as well as the health and well-being of the people, require the harnessing and proper utilization of the vast energy that is represented by the great rivers of India, which is not only largely running to waste but is often the cause of great injury to the land and the people who live on it. River commissions should be constituted to undertake this task in order to promote irrigation and ensure an even and continuous supply of water, to prevent disastrous floods and soil erosion, to eradicate malaria, to develop hydro-electric power, and in other ways to help in raising the general standards of life, especially in the rural areas. The power resources of the country have to be developed rapidly in this and other ways in order to provide the necessary foundation for the growth of industry and agriculture.

Education of Masses

Adequate arrangements should be made for the education of the masses with a view to raising them intellectually, economically, culturally and morally, and to fit them for the new forms of work and services which will open out before them. Public health services which are essential for the growth of the nation should be provided for on the widest scale, and in this, as in other matters, the needs of the rural areas should receive special attention. These should include special provisions for maternity and child welfare.

"Conditions should thus be created in which every individual has an equal opportunity for advance in every field of national activity and there is social security for all.

Science, in its innumerable fields of activity, has played an ever-increasing part in influencing and moulding human life and will do so in even greater measure in the future. Industrial, agricultural and cultural advance, as well as national defence, depend upon it. Scientific search is therefore a basic and essential activity of the State and should be organized and encouraged on the widest scale.

Safeguard for Labour

In regard to labour, the state shall safeguard the interests of industrial workers and shall secure for them a minimum wage and a decent standard of living, proper housing, hours of work and conditions of labour in conformity, as far as economic conditions in the country permit, with international standards, suitable machinery for the settlement of disputes between employees and workmen, and protection against the economic consequences of old age, sickness and unemployment. Workers shall have the right to form unions to protect their interests.

Rural indebtedness has in the past crushed the agricultural population, and though owing to various causes in recent years this has grown less, the burden still continues and must be removed, cheap credit must be made available through co-operatives. Co-operatives should also be organised for other purposes both in rural and urban areas. In particular, industrial co-operatives should be encouraged as being especially suited for the development of small-scale industry on a democratic basis.

While the immediate and urgent problems of India can only be effectively tackled by a joint and planned attack on all fronts – political, economic, agricultural, industrial and social – certain needs are of paramount importance today. Owing to the gross incompetence and mismanagement of the Government an incredible amount of suffering has been caused to the people of India. Millions have died of starvation, and scarcity of food and clothing is still widespread. Corruption in the services and in all matters pertaining to the supply and control of the vital necessaries of life is rampant and has become intolerable. These urgent problems require immediate attention.

International Affairs

In international affairs the Congress stands for the establishment of a world federation of free nations. Till such time as such a federation takes shape, India must develop friendly relations with all nations and particularly with her neighbours. In the Far East, in South-East Asia and in Western Asia, India has had trade and cultural relations for thousands of years and it is inevitable that with freedom she should renew and develop these relations. Reasons of security and future trends of trade also demand closer contacts with these regions. India, which has conducted her own struggle for freedom on a non-violent basis, will always throw her weight on the side of world peace and co-operation. She will also champion the freedom of all other subject nations and peoples for only on the basis of this freedom and the elimination of imperialism everywhere can world peace be established.

On the 8th of August 1942, the All India Congress Committee passed a resolution, since then famous in India's story. By its demands and challenge the Congress stands today. It is on the basis of this resolution and with its battle-cry that the Congress faces the elections.

Only thing that Counts

"The Congress, therefore, appeals to the voters all over the country to support Congress candidates in every way at the forthcoming elections, and to stand by the Congress at this critical juncture, which is so pregnant with future possibilities. In these elections, petty issues do not count, nor do individuals, nor sectarian cries – only one thing counts: the freedom and independence of our motherland, from which all other freedoms will flow to our people. Many a time the people of India have taken the pledge of independence; that pledge has yet to be redeemed, and the well-beloved cause for which it stands and which has summoned us so often, still beckons to us. The time is coming when we shall redeem it in full. This election is a small test for us, a preparation for the greater things to come. Let all those who care and long for freedom and the independence of India meet this test with strength and confidence and march together to the free India of our dreams."

Document No. 71

LETTER FROM LORD LAWRENCE TO MAULANA AZAD

India Office, London,
21 December, 1945

Dear Maulana Sahib,

You will, I am sure, be aware that a small delegation of Members of Parliament is coming to India for the purpose of making personal contacts. The Government here have felt that it is a great disadvantage in present circumstances that there has been so little touch between individuals in public life in this country and those in India during the last six years, and that there would be great advantages to both sides in such contacts being renewed. This is the basic idea of this delegation. They will come as individuals and they are not empowered in any way to act on behalf of the Government. On the other hand their impressions will of course be passed on by them to Ministers and others in Parliament.

I write therefore to express the hope that you may be able to meet Members of the delegation and discuss matters with them. I am sure that they will very much appreciate any such opportunity for a conversation with you.

I am writing a similar letter to Mr. Jinnah.

All the season's greetings to you.

Pathick Lawrence

Maulana Abul Kalam Azad,
Calcutta

Document No. 72

LETTER FROM SARDAR PATEL TO MAULANA AZAD

21 December, 1945

My dear Maulana Sahib,

I received your telegram of the 19th inst. yesterday evening. I have already sent a cheque for Rs. 50,000, but I am afraid we are wasting good money for nothing and Congress reputation will in the end suffer badly. I am enclosing herewith a Press cutting from which you will see what type of candidates are being put up by the Ahrar Party in the Punjab for whom they want our help. From this cutting you will see that immediately the League candidates' nominations were declared invalid, the Ahrar candidates, who remained on the scene and whose nominations were declared valid, joined the Muslim League. It is very sad that such candidates are chosen to oppose the League. In any case it is very unwise that we should be mixed up with such a shady transaction. I would still request you to reconsider the whole position and withhold the help. May I again remind you that my information is that the Ahrars will get no place except one or two in the Punjab?

I am afraid we have mishandled the whole Punjab situation. We have to fight the Akalis as there has been no settlement as was expected and we will not get more than 5 or 6 seats after a good deal of expense which could be easily avoided.

Please excuse me for bringing these facts to your notice, but I have done so as I have been considerably oppressed by a feeling of failure in duty at a critical juncture in one of the most important provinces in these elections. I do not wish to blame anybody but I do feel that if we continue to handle affairs in the same fashion, we will suffer a serious defeat in spite of such huge expenditure and a good deal of time and energy being spent over it.

I trust your health has improved.

My attention has just been drawn to a press report from Nagpur wherein a very mischievous account has appeared about the election of the party leader in the Central Assembly. You must have noticed it also. It appears in the *Hindustan Standard* of the 20th inst.

Yours sincerely,
Vallabhbhai

Maulana Abul Kalam Azad,
Calcutta

Document No. 73

TELEGRAM FROM PANDIT NEHRU TO MAULANA ABUL KALAM AZAD

1945

RECEIVED YOUR MESSAGE AT ONE AFTERNOON. IN OBEDIENCE DIRECTIONS WORKING COMMITTEE. AM PREPARED RETURN IMMEDIATELY ON UNDERSTANDING COME BACK KASHMIR LATER. EARLY RETURN ONLY POSSIBLE BY AEROPLANE FROM SRINAGAR. NO SERVICE PLANES AVAILABLE SRINAGAR OR PINDI. AM UNDER DETENTION AND CAN MAKE NO ARRANGEMENTS. SHALL AWAIT FACILITIES FOR RETURN.

JAWAHARLAL

Document No. 74

CONGRESS WORKING COMMITTEES RESOLUTION ON INDONESIA WITH MAULANA AZAD AS PRESIDENT

1945

The Working Committee have watched with admiration and sympathy the valiant struggle in defence of their newly won republic and independence which the people of Indonesia have been carrying on with steadfast courage and determination against British and Dutch forces. This Committee emphatically condemn the wanton invasion of Jawa and other parts of Indonesia in order to impose Dutch imperialist domination on their inhabitants against their unanimous demand for a free State. Any support from any quarter to imperialist designs in Indonesia, Indo-China and elsewhere is resented throughout Asia as culpable violation of the professed aims of the United Nations and the undeniable right of Asian nationals. This will destroy the chance of international understanding and the very basis of any future world organization. The Committee regret that the United States of America have by their passive attitude encouraged these imperialist aggressions. While expressing thier heartfelt sympathy with the Indonesia and Indo-Chinese nationalists for the enormous loss and suffering inflicted upon them by the imperialist powers, this Committee are particularly distressed to find the units of the Indian army arrayed against the Indonesians and Indo-Chinese and view with deep indignation this mischievous misuse of the Indian forces by the British Government. This Committee note with resentment that the Government of India has not granted necessary facilities to enable Jawaharlal Nehru to proceed to Java in response to Dr. Sockarno's invitation and reaffirm their determination to put an end to India's political subjection to which the present intolerable state of humiliating helplessness is due.

Document No. 75

LETTER FROM SARDAR PATEL TO MAULANA AZAD

1 January, 1946

My dear Maulana Sahib,

Your telegram was received yesterday for sending a lakh of rupees to Sitaram Sekhseria, and I have immediately made arrangements by telephone accordingly. In the press I read yesterday that Shamsuddin Ahmed has resigned from the Krishak Praja Party and joined the Muslim League. It is difficult to rely upon anybody. This gentleman was meeting me at Calcutta and assuring me about securing a large number of seats if help was given.

In the Punjab, the two parties are still quarrelling with increasing vigour. If Maulana Daud engages his personal secretary for election work from one party, the other party wants him to keep another from their party. These quarrels have been encouraged and it has a very demoralising effect on the general situation. I have got a wire from Maulana Daud today asking me to send Pandit Jawaharlal to the Punjab for nearly two weeks. I do not understand how this can be done and what advantage one could gain by such tours. At present Jawaharlal is going to Sind. His tours create a lot of enthusiasm and huge crowds gather together, but these demonstrations have no value for the purpose of election, as they influence no voters in the Muslim constituencies. The Hindu voters need no encouragement.

I have sent you a telegram this morning suggesting that the Election Board meeting should be kept on the 17th and the Assembly Party meeting should be kept on the 18th. I would have kept it earlier but as some members are not free till the 18th, I have suggested that date.

Apparently you were detained at Calcutta longer than expected. So your stay at Bindhachal will again be interrupted by the Delhi meeting. It is possible that we may not get proposals from all the provinces by that time. The Andhra Provincial Congress Committee has already asked for more time.

Rajaji's affair has been settled, for the time being, and if both parties abide by it loyally, things may improve.

I hope you will improve by the change.

Yours sincerely,
Vallabhbhai Patel

Maulana Abul Kalam Azad,
Bindhachal

Document No. 76

LETTER FROM SARDAR PATEL TO MAULANA AZAD

2 January, 1946

My dear Maulana Sahib,

I received your letter of 2nd inst. today.

I am receiving complaints regarding the Punjab nominations even now but we can do nothing in the matter at this stage. You must also be receiving such complaints.

Maulvi Gani has come here from Ludhiana and he wants financial help for the Provincial Assembly elections. He has not been authorised by anybody, but he is a member of the election board. Last week I got letters from Maulana Daud and Dr. Gopichand asking for financial help. Yesterday I got a telphone message from Sjt. Bhim Sen Sachar and he wants me to send Rs. 5 lakh. Today I have got a telegram saying that they are sending Seth Sudarshan for this purpose. This is a telegram signed by both Sjt. Sachar and Maulana Daud. Even in their demands they are not united and different people make different demands. Their estimates differ violently. In these circumstances to render proper help becomes so difficult that one does not know what to do. However, I am trying my best to help them.

It seems impossible now to make any settlement with the Akalis, and perhaps we must wait till the results are out.

I am surprised to read the last two paragraphs of your letter about the Bengal situation. I have done nothing there without your consultation and approval. I first wrote you a letter from Poona for the framing of a budget in consultation with Prafulla Babu, Sarat Babu and Kiran Babu. You four sat together and sent me the budget. After that I came to Calcutta and we formed the election board, after our work was over, and this was done with your full approval. When I left Calcutta, I gave the secretary of the board Rs. 50,000 and informed him of what I had given to you before. Nothing more was done by me and I know nothing of any finance committee being constituted there by anybody. For the first time I hear about it from you. I only told the board that for the proper spending of the help that I may be called upon to give, I will hold them responsible. That was natural because of our experience in the Central Assembly elections.

I do not know what method you devised for smooth working in Calcutta and you have never told me anything about it.

A Muslim board was formed after I left, of which I was not informed. Shamsuddin, the secretary of this board, joined the League immediately after that. This I have learnt from the newspapers. Another gentleman has been appointed in his place.

My information, according to reports from Bengal, is that we can expect no more than about 8 to 10 Muslim seats. The rest will all go to the League. In my opinion, the proper course all over India would have been to contest the elections on Congress tickets. The independent machinery will give us no more seats in Bengal, but I have subordinated my opinion in these matters both in the Punjab and in Bengal and elsewhere to yours without question. Therefore, I do not know why you suggest that any finance committee has been appointed by me or that you have devised any method and that nothing would be achieved by that method and no appreciable result would be produced.

I wired you for approval to fix meetings in Delhi on the 18th and 19th. In reply your telegram came stating that you are arranging these meetings on those dates. I have not yet seen anything in the Press about it, nor do I know whether invitations have been issued or not.

Yours sincerely,
Vallabhbhai Patel

Maulana Abul Kalam Azad,
Bindhachal

Document No. 77

LETTER FROM MAULANA AZAD TO SARDAR PATEL

Bindhachal,
2 January, 1946

My dear Vallabhbhai,

I had received your last letter in Calcutta. Before my departure I had sent a telegram to you to send money to Sitaram Seksaria. I hope you have arranged the needful.

The affairs of the Punjab are in a muddle for the last several years. The only remedy was to release the Congress from the contending parties and infuse fresh blood in it. But when I went and studied the situation on the spot, I felt that it was difficult to bring forward new men just at that time. Therefore, there was no way out but to keep the old element there, and to let in the new element to a certain extent as a balancing power till fresh elections of the Congress are held. I think that there could be no other method for the time being, and I hold the same opinion even now.

I had advised Dr. Gopichand and Ghaznavi, when I was in Lahore, that if the Akalis left 16 or 17 seats for the Congress, they should not contest the remaining seats, and they could make a settlement with them on that basis. I have been giving them the same advice after my return from Lahore. In Calcutta too we directed them on the same lines; so much so that I told Ghaznavi on his departure from Calcutta to give up a few (2 or 3) more seats if there could be a settlement on that basis. But the fact is that the Akalis were not prepared to make any concession or settlement.

If we totally ignore Congressite Sikhs, the result would be that the Congress will lose all hold among the Sikhs, which is impossible for us to do.

I fully appreciate your opinion about the Ahrars. No one has yet reached here on their behalf. I shall not do anything in this respect unless I am fully satisfied with the situation.

Now I want to say a few words about the Bengal situation. I learnt after your departure from Calcutta that you have constituted a finance committee with full powers to do what they deem fit. Had I know that before, I would not have remained in the dark and would have adopted the necessary attitude.

I tried to devise a method of smooth working in Calcutta, but now I find that nothing would be achieved by this method, and all attempts would produce no appreciable result.

Yours sincerely,
A.K. Azad

Sardar Vallabhbhai Patel,
68 Marine Drive,
Bombay

Document No. 78

TELEGRAM FROM MAULANA AZAD TO SARDAR PATEL

BINDHACHAL,
6 JANUARY, 1946

SARDAR PATEL,
BOMBAY

ALL PROVINCES EMPHASISE INABILITY MAKING NEW COMMITTEE UP TO APRIL. JAWAHARLAL AND KRIPALANI FAVOUR REMOVING ANNUAL SESSION ONE MONTH FURTHER. I SUGGEST FIFTEENTH MAY BOMBAY. WIRE YOUR OPINION.

ABUL KALAM AZAD

Document No. 79

LETTER FROM SARDAR PATEL TO MAULANA AZAD

8 January, 1946

My dear Maulana Sahib,

I have received a letter from the Frontier where people want you for a couple of days in order to counteract whatever mischief that may have been done by Mr. Jinnah's visit there. I do not know whether you will be able to respond, particularly because of your health.

Yesterday I got a telegram from you suggesting the holding of the Congress a month later than the announced programme, and also the change of venue from Delhi to Bombay. I am afraid the postponement of the Congress for a month will drive us into heart of the hot season and would be very inconvenient to all. However, I have consulted the Bombay people and they are willing to undertake the responsibility if it is so decided, but the decision must be taken without delay.

I have received a telegram from Asaf Ali this morning that the Delhi People want to stick to their decision of holding it there.

Seth Sudarshan had come here and so had Gilani. They had a frank talk in my presence. Some sort of understanding between the Akalis and the Congress appears to be possible and they have drafted some tentative proposals which they will take to Maulana Daud and the Akali Party there. If they will agree, settlement may secure us about 16 seats from the Sikh constituencies, and perhaps improve the atmosphere.

Sudarshan has brought a letter for a demand of money which is very large. He wants Rs. 6 lakh and that demand is now supported by Maulana Daud. The previous day Maulvi Gani had come to me. His demand was that two lakhs would fully meet with their requirements. On that day I had a letter from Dr. Gopichand. He thought that a lakh and a half would be sufficient. These conflicting demands make our work difficult. For the present I have sent them one lakh and have asked them to sit together and send me a joint demand agreed upon by all of them. If they agree, I will try my best to help them, but it is difficult to make them agree.

Yours sincerely,
Vallabhbhai Patel

Maulana Abul Kalam Azad,
Bindhachal

Document No. 80

LETTER FROM MAULANA AZAD TO PATHICK LAWRENCE

19-A, Ballygunj,
Circular Road,

Calcutta, 14 January, 1946

Dear Lord Pethick-Lawrence,

I have to thank you for your letter of 21st December 1945, sent through the Governor of Bengal.

I agree with you that personal contacts are of mutual advantage, and I shall be glad to meet members of the delegation at the first convenient opportunity.

With kind regards,

Yours sincerely,
A.K. Azad

Maulana Abul Kalam Azad,
Armsdell,
Simla

Document No. 81

LETTER FROM SARDAR PATEL TO MAULANA AZAD

Bombay,
11 February, 1946

My dear Maulana Sahib,

I have not heard from you since you left Karachi. About your proposal to the League, its reaction can be seen from the attached cutting from the League's mouthpiece in Calcutta.

I am keeping the committee meeting from the 16th to consider proposals received from Nagpur, Andhra, Tamil Nadu, Kerala and Orissa. It will take more than a week to dispose of these applications. I am afraid it will be a very troublesome job, but there is no other way. I have invited the members of the committee, but I doubt whether anybody except Sjt. Shankarrao will come here. The nomination dates are coming very near and I must finish them.

Please let me know what has been done in Assam.

Haji Moula Bux is coming here tomorrow and if there is anything to report, I will write to you.

When are you going to the Punjab? The elections there will soon be over and you will have to be there in time.

The food situation in the country has been very badly handled by the Government. The position is getting more serious. The Viceroy is recommending cutting down of rations which are already not enough to sustain a normal human being. He has invited Bapu and Jinnah. Bapu is not in a position to go there, because of the strain on his health in Madras. I understand the Viceroy's Secretary will see him at Sevagram. He wants, probably the public to co-operate in cutting down rations. How can public support a proposal which would result in starving the people?

I forgot to inform you that while I was at Karachi a demand for money came from Calcutta and my son has already remitted a very large portion of the budgeted amount.

Hope you are doing well.

Yours sincerely,
Vallabhbhai Patel

Maulana Abul Kalam Azad

Document No. 82

TELEGRAM FROM MAULANA AZAD TO SARDAR PATEL

CALCUTTA,
14 FEBRUARY, 1946

SARDAR VALLABHBHAI PATEL,
BOMBAY

YOUR MESSAGE[1] AND TELEGRAM. ATTENDING MEETING IF POSSIBLE. BOARD MAY DISPOSE NOMINATIONS REMAINING PROVINCES AFTER WHICH I SHALL DISPOSE APPEALS IF ANY

ABUL KALAM AZAD

---

1. See Enclosure.

Enclosure

Sardar Patel's Message for Maulana Azad

YOUR TELEGRAM. THERE CAN BE NO APPEAL AGAINST CENTRAL BOARD'S DECISION. BESIDES, SUCH A COURSE WOULD ENCOURAGE INDISCIPLINE AND ENDLESS DISPUTES. BEST COURSE FOR YOU IS TO FLY TO BOMBAY FROM DELHI. BAPU ALSO WILL BE IN BOMBAY ON THE 18TH AND 19TH. PUNJAB ELECTIONS BEING DELAYED. YOU ARE NOT WANTED THERE TILL 25TH. PLEASE REPLY.

DR. CHOITHRAM AND NICHALDAS ARE MEETING YOU AT DELHI AND CONVEYING ALL INFORMATION INCLUDING MR. (G.M.) SYED'S INTERVIEW WITH GOVERNOR. HE HAS VIOLATED PARLIAMENTARY CONVENTION AND ISSUED PRESS NOTE CONTAINING FALSE STATEMENTS. ALSO ACTED AGAINST THE VICEROY'S PROMISE TO YOU THAT GOVERNORS WILL DEAL FAIRLY AND NOT INTERFERE. PUBLIC MEETING GIVING THREATS IMMEDIATELY AFTER FORMATION OF MINISTRY PRESIDED OVER BY LIAQUAT ENCOURAGES VIOLENCE AND TROUBLE. VICEROY MAY BE INFORMED ACCORDINGLY.

Document No. 83

LETTER FROM MAULANA AZAD TO SARDAR PATEL

Shillong,
15.2.46

My dear Vallabhbhai,

I caught fever on my arrival at Shillong, which is still persisting.

The differences between the Assam Valley and the Surma Valley have gone deep in Assam, and now every question is viewed from the same point of view. The rivalry of these groups went on in regard to Ministry also, and as you know, other groups had their demands too. However, I have tried that these sentiments may not surge up any further, so that the demands of various groups as well as the efficiency of the Cabinet may not suffer. A great deal of success has, therefore, been achieved, and so far as I could gauge, I have found that the whole province was satisfied and happy over it. Basanto Babu has been taken in the Ministry, Mr. Sarma has been nominated for Speakership from the Assam Valley, who will prove a suitable person for it.

Only one man, Abdul Mutalib, out of the three Nationalist Muslims returned to the legislature, deserved to be included in the Ministry. He has, therefore, been taken. The remaining two seats have been kept vacant. Saadullah has been told that if he co-operates with the Congress Party work and its parliamentary programme then the Congress will gladly include two of his men in the Ministry. I have prepared Saadullah for this, but Jinnah will probably not agree to such a proposal. However, we have clarified our position.

On my arrival here I got the message of the Viceroy that he desired to meet me. If I get fit I shall leave for Delhi on the 15th. After which I may have to go to Peshawar and Lahore. Under the circumstances it is difficult for me to get time to go to Bombay. You have called the Parliamentary Board on the 16th. It should finish the work of the remaining provinces. If any appeal will be filed in this connection, you would send it to me and I will decide it in consultation with you.

Yours sincerely,
Abul Kalam Azad

Sardar Vallabhbhai Patel,
Bombay

Document No. 84

LETTER FROM MAULANA AZAD TO SARDAR PATEL

Calcutta,
19 February, 1946

My dear Vallabhbhai,

I caught fever on my arrival at Shillong, which is still persisting.

The differences between the Assam Valley and the Surma Valley have gone deep in Assam, and now every question is viewed from the same point of view. The rivalry of these groups went on in regard to Ministry also, and as you know, other groups had their demands too. However, I have tried that these sentiments may not surge up any further, so that the demands of various groups as well as the efficiency of the Cabinet may not suffer. A great deal of success has, therefore, been achieved, and so far as I could gauge, I have found that the whole province was satisfied and happy over it. Basanto Babu has been taken in the Ministry, Mr. Sarma has been nominated for Speakership from the Assam Valley, who will prove a suitable person for it.

Only one man, Abdul Mutalib, out of the three Nationalist Muslims returned to the legislature, deserved to be included in the Ministry. He has, therefore, been taken. The remaining two seats have been kept vacant. Sir Mohammad Sadullah[1] has been told that if he co-operates with the Congress Party to work out its parliamentary programme, then the Congress will gladly include two of his men in the Ministry. I have prepared Sadullah for this, but Jinnah will probably not agree to such a proposal. However, we have clarified our position.

On my arrival here I got a message of the Viceroy that he desired to meet me. If I get fit I shall leave for Delhi on the 15th. After which I may have to go to Peshawar and Lahore. Under the circumstances it is difficult for me to get time to go to Bombay. You have called the Parliamentary Board on the 16th. It should finish the work of the remaining provinces. If any appeal will be filed in this connection, you would send it to me, and I will decide it in consultation with you.

Yours sincerely,
A.K. Azad

Sardar Vallabhbhai Patel,
Congress House,
Bombay

---

1. Muslim League leader of Assam; member of Assam Governor's Executive Council before Provincial autonomy; appointed Prime Minister of Assam after resignation of Congress Ministry in 1939.

Document No. 85

LETTER FROM SARDAR PATEL TO MAULANA AZAD

Bombay,
23 February, 1946

My dear Maulana Sahib,

In continuation of our telephonic conversation yesterday. I feel bound to make it clear that the nomination of Sjt. Pandey is nothing but an unexpected letting down of the Central Board and a total disregard of ordinary courtesy. If you wanted to change the decision, you should have at least consulted us. The analogy of the change in the U.P. decisions is not at all applicable here. That question was settled at the time when the decisions were taken by the Board and the matter was left open in certain cases; even there it was decided that nothing is to be done without consulting the provincial leaders, including Pantji, one of the members of the Board concerned. In Mahakoshal no such reservation was made. There can be no appeal against the decision of the Board, including you as Chairman, and if such authority were vested in you, there should have been a specific provision in the Working Committee's Resolution. Besides, if you were the appellate authority, you cannot at the same time be the Chairman of the Board, whose decisions are appealable to you alone. This is a strange procedure and your action has lowered our prestige in the eyes of the people of that province. I enclose herewith a copy of a letter received from R.S. Shuklaji[1], who was also not consulted by you. I had issued a public statement that the decisions of Mahakoshal are final and are not appealable and hence there will be no change. You referred to certain documents in your telephonic conversation, which were shown to me also. Sjt. Chedilal was here and he had explained to me about it. Sjt. Pandey was also here and I had seen Sjt. Kishorelal Mashruwalla.[2] They were informed that there will be no change. I had not the slightest idea that they will come to you and get a reversal of the Board's decision. If I had known that they were to come to you, I would have written to you about it. I had also seen your Press Statement to the effect that these decisions were final. If you had taken all the powers alone and disposed of all the nominations, nobody would have been more glad than myself. The procedure adopted in this case is such that I cannot understand it at all.

From your conversation on the phone, I also understood that my coming to Lahore is likely to embarrass you and that I should rather not go there. But for Maulana Daud's invitation to go there, I would not have agreed to do so, particularly in my present state of health. In Sind also, I went there because a special messenger came to call me simultaneously when another came to Delhi to call you. If you had expressed the slightest desire that I should not go, I would have agreed with the greatest pleasure. But I feel from your conversation that I have lost your confidence and therefore you don't want me to go there. I do not wish to say anything about what has been represented to you and about the group that has given you that impression but the least that I could do in the circumstances is that in view of your attitude I propose to immediately tender my resignation from the Central Board as well as the Working Committee. I should be grateful if you will relieve me without any delay as my continuance in the present state is likely to give me constant mental trouble and anxiety. I regret very much to say that I have to take this action at a very critical juncture but I feel that the treatment that has been given to me is, to say the least, unexpected and undeserved and hence no alternative is left to me.

Yours sincerely,
Vallabhbhai Patel

Maulana Abul Kalam Azad,
C/O Frontier PCC,
Peshawar

---

1. Entered Legislative Council of Central Provinces in 1923 as member of Swaraj Party; Minister of Education, July 1937; Premier, August 1938; Chief Minister of CP after Independence and later of reformed State of Madhya Pradesh until 1956.

2. Exponent of Gandhian Philosophy; editor, *Young India*, and *Harijan*; member, Zakir Husain Committee on Basic Education.

Document No. 86

TELEGRAM FROM MAULANA AZAD TO SARDAR PATEL

PESHAWAR,
23 FEBRUARY, 1946

SARDAR VALLABHBHAI PATEL,
BOMBAY

WOULD BE EXTREMELY HELPFUL IF YOU COULD KINDLY COME LAHORE. OTHERWISE DO FLY TO DELHI AT LEAST STAYING DELHI 25TH-26TH.

ABULKALAMAZAD

Document No. 87

LETTER FROM MAULANA AZAD TO SARDAR PATEL

Camp Lahore,
28 February, 1946

My dear Vallabhbhai,

I have received your letter of 23 February 1946. I am extremely sorry that you were put to so much trouble owing to this affair. I assure you that I had not viewed this matter in the light you have taken it, nor was I under the slightest impression that I am taking a decision against the decision of the Board. You are aware that I had received appeals of certain candidates for the Central Assembly as well, and there was a case about which I had personal knowledge and I held quite a contrary view about it to that of the decision of the Board. Nevertheless, I did not like to take any action on it, more than that I apprised you of my impressions. And when you replied that a change would be improper, I accepted your view unhesitatingly, and rejected the appeal. Under the circumstances it is obvious that there could be no reason for me to adopt a different attitude in this matter, or would have knowingly desired to undermine the prestige of the Board. You can never expect such a thing from me.

We are working together for the last 26 years in perfect unison. Every morning and evening of our public life has passed in amity and concord. We should not hurry in forming opinions against one another. I always expect a generous attitude from you and other co-workers, and (I) think that I deserve it.

The whole affair is detailed below:

We had made final selections of the candidates of several provinces in Delhi. But at the same time complaints were received from the candidates that the provincial Boards had not published or informed them of their decisions before, and therefore they said that they did not get an opportunity to appeal to the Central Board, if they wanted to do so. We had felt the weight of these complaints and had formed the opinion that we will reconsider on appeal special cases deserving a revision of the Delhi selections. Accordingly 30 appeals were received from U.P., and out of them I admitted eleven and changed the previous decision.

Like U.P., telegrams and letters of protest began to pour in from Mahakoshal also. Every letter complained that the provincial board had not made its decisions public, and the list was published in the local papers only on 5 February, and therefore they wanted to have a chance for appeal. I did not take any notice of the complaints. But when I returned from Shillong, this new appeal came before me, and I had occasion to go through all the papers and the circumstances. I was totally unaware of the fact that the case had already been considered by you, nor I came across any statement from you about the finality of decisions about Mahakoshal. On considering the appeal I concluded that sheer injustice was done to the appellant. Even then I did not give my decision immediately. I wired to the provincial board and awaited a reply for five days. As no satisfactory reply was received, I decided the case according to my judgment. Had you informed me in time, I would certainly have not liked to interfere.

I tell you once again that I am really very sorry over this situation, and assure you that whatever was done was due to the fact that I did not know of any announcement of the Board in this respect.

Appeals are still pouring in from Madras and Andhra; but I have given a statement to the Press that the appeals will be heard no more.

Yours sincerely,
A.K. Azad

Sardar Vallabhbhai Patel,
Congress House,
Bombay

Document No. 88

LETTER FROM DR. RAJENDRA PRASAD TO MAULANA ABUL KALAM AZAD

Sadaquat Ashram,
P.O. Dighaghat, Patna,

2 March, 1946

My dear Maulana Saheb,

Polling begins in Bihar on 2nd March in the Muslim constituencies and in the non-Mahomedan constituencies on the 4th and goes on up to the 9th. The results would be known a few days later. There is no serious contest in the non-Muslim constituencies except in the districts of Ranchi and Singhbhum where the Adibasis (aborigines) are putting up a severe fight and in one or two other places. Of the 40 Muslim seats one reserved for women has gone to the League because the nomination paper of the Jamiat candidate was rejected. There is serious contest in the remaining 38 seats. Friends and workers report to me that the Jamiat, Momins and the Congress are expected to get 15 to 20 seats. It is, however, best to wait for the counting of votes.

I expect that some time in the third week of this month the Leader of the Congress Party may be called to form a ministry, Bihar will be the first province which has remained under Section 93 since 1939 to be called upon to form a Congress Ministry. I gather from your statement and the action that has been taken in the Frontier and Assam that the Congress Party would accept office although there is no decision of the Working Committee or the A.I.C.C. to that effect that I know, I think it is desirable that definite instruction should be given and line of action laid down. The Cabinet Ministers will also be arriving in India towards the end of this month.

I think that all this necessitates a meeting of the Working Committee unless something was settled in Calcutta at the time of drawing up the election manifesto and you have only to issue instruction. In any case, we should have definite instruction whether we should accept office. It is also necessary to know whether the old resolution of the Working Committee fixing the salary of Ministers at five hundred with some allowance for car and house still stands. The ministries will have immediately to tackle the very serious problem of food and a common policy, as far as possible, would be desirable. I also apprehend that soon after our people take office trouble will arise in many places particularly in labour areas where strikes may take place. We should have some clear idea about these and a lot of other similar matters. I know the elections will go on till April and some of the members of the Working Committee may not available but I consider it desirable to have a meeting of the Working Committee soon so that instruction may be given as regards the general line to be pursued by our people in office. I shall be obliged for any instruction which you may think it necessary to communicate.

Yours sincerely,
Rajendra Prasad

P.S. I am posting this letter both to Delhi and Calcutta.

Document No. 89

LETTER FROM SARDAR PATEL TO MAULANA AZAD

Bombay,
6 March, 1946

My dear Maulana Sahib,

I have received your letter of 28 February today.

I know that you had received appeals of certain candidates for the Central Assembly and in one case you differed from the decision of the Board but at that time also I had made it clear that no appeal can be entertained by you on the decisions of the Board. I do not know how you have got such an idea even now. I may also bring to your notice that in that particular case, the papers were circulated amongst the members of the Board who were not likely to attend and they had sent their opinion. You were also informed that the proposal of Sjt. Bhargava in that case was strongly supported by Sjt. Asaf Ali, who had personal knowledge about the merits of the candidates concerned. You had not sent your opinion in time and the Board finally decided after consulting Maulana Daud in Poona. This decision was announced and also communicated to the candidate concerned. Supporters of the rejected candidate approached you at Calcutta and you insisted on a change till the last moment on the ground of your having received an appeal.

You did not conceal your resentment against the decision of the Board and gave vent to your feelings when we met at Calcutta, in the presence of some of the interested parties, but I thought it better to keep quiet at that time. You are certainly entitled to claim a generous attitude from us and I have done my best to do so, but you must also make allowance for an honest difference of opinion. You cannot insist that your opinion is the only correct one. In the Punjab we honestly held different opinions but you have never recognised that there is scope for such a difference of opinion in that matter and you have missed no opportunity to remind us about it.

You are certainly entitled to a generous attitude from us; personally I have done my best to do so. In the Punjab I have differed strongly from you in the matter of the election campaign on many points, including the question of financial help to be given to the Congress Party. I was expected to help them only in the matter of Muslim constituencies. In this they have lost all (along) the line and I knew that they were going to lose. They insisted on financial help being given for non-Muslim constituencies and tried to put pressure on me through you. I have agreed without hesitation to whatever you suggested in this connection. They have avoided all responsibility but as you were all working against heavy odds, I thought it my duty to accept your suggestions without question. In the matter of selection of candidates in the Punjab also, we had differences but we have endorsed everything that you have done without the slightest hesitation.

No doubt there were complaints received by you from various provinces but they were received by us also. I may be permitted to say that these appeals and protests have been encouraged by an impression that has been created all over that the President can hear appeals over the decisions of the Board. Somehow or other, you have held that idea in spite of my protests from the time of the Central Assembly elections.

In the U.P. the position was different and I have already written to you about it in my last letter. In the case of the CP your decision has been arbitrary and *ex-parte*. I have already sent you a copy of Shuklaji's letter from which you must have seen that he was assured by me several times that the decisions of the Central Board in Mahakoshal were final and not liable to any change. You were a party to the decision and there was no reservation for reconsideration or review, nor was any notice given to us about the proposed change.

Your non-interference in the matter of appeals pouring in from Madras and Andhra referred to in your letter cannot in any manner justify the arbitrary and *ex-parte* decision in Mahakoshal ignoring the Board altogether. I am afraid you have not realised the ridiculous position in which we are placed in the whole of that province.

Perhaps it may be that your approach to these questions is different from mine and therefore it is difficult for me to understand or appreciate it. It would therefore be better to relieve me from this embarrassing position altogether, as early as possible.

Yours sincerely,
Vallabhbhai Patel

Maulana Abul Kalam Azad,
President,
Indian National Congress,
New Delhi

Document No. 90

WORKING COMMITTEE'S RESOLUTIONS WITH AZAD AS PRESIDENT

The following is the text of the four resolutions of the Working Committee passed on 15th and 16th March, 1946, at Bombay.

I
Resolution on Food

Whereas, the war and its after-effects have already created a serious food situation which has been materially aggravated by the failure of rains in many parts of India, with the result that the country is faced with both a food and a cloth famine, it is essential that the policy of the Government and the people should be one at this time of crisis. Hunger makes no distinction between high and low, Hindu and Muslim, or any other. But the real burden of suffering, however, will inevitably fall on the poor. In the circumstances, the Working Committee would like to make its policy clear.

The first thing in these difficult times is for the people not to lose heart. Everyone should realize his personal duty and perform it to the best of his ability, believing that if everyone acts likewise India will be able to save thousands of poor lives. Every villager and town's man should, therefore, do the best he can for his neighbour and for himself.

Everyone who possesses any land should in the shortest time grow such foodstuffs on it as he can. Cultivable land lying waste should speedily be brought under the plough and every facility should be given for this purpose by the State. After fulfilling his own minimum requirements from his produce, he should make the remainder available for others who may be in need.

Preference should be given to food crops over money crops wherever practicable.

People should sink ordinary wells and dig tanks, wherever there is scarcity of water and all facilities for this purpose should be given by the State and local bodies.

It is the duty of the rich today to live simply and divert their energy and wealth towards productive and constructive activities for the relief of distress.

Every effort should be made to secure supplies from abroad, but we should not feel helpless in any case. On the contrary, we must produce all we can in India and be prepared to face all emergencies with the resources available. It must be remembered that even the receipt of additional imports or the raising of additional crops will not serve the purpose in view unless the supplies reach the starving places in time and are equitably distributed there.

All food should be economically used and expenditure on occasions of marriages and other ceremonies must be avoided.

Processes of canning and preservation of fruit should be encouraged and widely adopted so that full use may be made of all available fruit and no part thereof may be wasted.

It is the duty of the State to put all their available resources of manpower, technical skill and mechanical appliances, whether civil or military, for growing, preserving and transporting food wherever necessary. All exports of cereals, foodstuffs, oilseeds, oilcakes, groundnuts oil and other edibles should be absolutely prohibited.

The State should sink deep wells and adopt other means of water supply wherever necessary. Demobilized and discharged personnel from the defence services, including the I.N.A. should be utilized for increasing the production of foodstuffs.

The Committee expects the nation to make all necessary sacrifices for relieving distress in the country and for making successful any reasonable schemes of rationing and procurement any measures for checking hoarding, blackmarketing and corruption that may have to be taken on hand.

It is clear that just as it is the duty of the public to co-operate in all helpful ways, it is the primary duty of the Government to understand and fulfil the essential needs of the people. Measures for meeting the serious situation cannot be fully successful and effective unless power vests in the people.

So far as want of cloth is concerned, it is the duty of the State and the people alike to render every assistance to the villagers in order to enable them to produce by their own effort enough Khadi in the villages. The State should provide facilities for cotton-growing or cotton itself, and instruments of production and instructors where necessary.

Congress Committees and Congressmen are advised to help in every way to give effect to the recommendations in this resolution.

II
Resolution on the International situation

The Working Committee have noted with grave concern the growing tension in the international situation resulting in open recrimination between the great Powers and attempts on their part to secure or hold on to colonial areas and vantage points and create satellite States, which may lead to possible future conflicts. The war that has recently ended has, in spite of the professions made during the course of it, neither ended the imperialist domination of subject countries nor the era of power politics. The old imperialism still continues and in addition new types of imperialism are growing. The recent UNO Conference in London is startling evidence of the fact that instead of a new order of free and united nations evolving, there is disunity among the leading nations and lack of freedom over vast areas. Oil is still the lure of imperial domination, and security and preservation of the so called life-lines of empty or strategic outposts are made the excuses for expansion as well as retention of colonial areas. This continuation of the old and discredited policy which has led already to two disastrous world wars is likely to result in yet another war on a more colosal and destructive scale.

It is evident that peace and freedom cannot grow out of these seeds of continuing conflict and war. Imperialist policy has to be discarded not only in the interests of subject nations, but also to rid the world of the peril that might overwhelm humanity. It has thus become urgently necessary to end foreign domination over the countries of Asia and Africa, and for foreign armies to be withdrawn from all such countries, and notably from Indonesia, Manchuria, Indo-China, Iran and Egypt. India still remains the crux of the problem of Asian freedom and on the independence of India depends the freedom of many countries and the peace of the world.

III
Resolution on South Africa

The Working Committee of the Indian National Congress are of opinion that the disabilities of the Indian settlers in South Africa constitute a blot on humanity and a slur on the civilization of the West. As the submission to His Excellency the Viceroy of the Indian

Deputation from South Africa shows, the disabilities are an unbroken tale of progressive prejudice against Asiatics defined as "any Turk and any member of a race or tribe whose national home is in Asia but which does not include any member of the Jewish or the Syrian race or a person belonging to the race or class known as the Cape Malay," and of broken promises and declarations. A civilization that requires for its protection a series of legal enactments imposing political and economic restrictions on coloured and Asiatic peoples must contain seeds of future wars and its own destruction.

The Committee are of opinion that the contemplated breach of trade relations between India and the Union of South Africa is the mildest step that the Government of India could have taken. The Committee would ask the Government of India forthwith to withdraw their High Commissioner, if the Union Government would not suspend the proposed legislation, pending the convening of a Round Table Conference between the two governments to consider the whole policy of the Union Government against non-White peoples of the earth.

The Committee are painfully surprised to find Field Marshal Smuts, the Premier of the Union, dismissing, on the untenable plea of regarding the proposed anti-Asiatic bill as a domestic affair, the right of the Indian Government and, by parity of reasoning of the other Allied Powers, of friendly intervention. The Committee hold that at this time of the day it is not open to any State, however powerful it may be, to refuse to listen to the public opinion of the world as voiced through its different states with reference to any legislation regarded by them as of an inhuman character or as amounting to a slur on the self-respect of the races comprising such a State.

The Committee venture to advise the victorious Allies to take notice of the contemplated action of the Government of South Africa inasmuch as the late war would have been fought in vain if now the persistence by the Union Government of South Africa in the bar sinister against Asiatic races and coloured people inhabiting that sub-continent is maintained.

To the Indian Deputation from South Africa the Committee would say that whilst they (the Committee) and, indeed, the whole of India, irrespective of parties or communities, are with them in their just struggle and would lend them all the moral weight they can, they should realize that the brunt of the unequal struggle will have to be borne by them, and the Committee feel assured that the

Indians in South Africa will worthily carry out the example set by them years ago of vindicating their self-respect and that of the Motherland by the noble rule of self-suffering.

The Committee would, however, fain hope, even at the eleventh hour, that in the place of the indefensible law of the jungle, which the policy as revealed by the contemplated legislation enunciates, the Government of the Union of South Africa and its White settlers would listen to reason and the appeal of the moral law by which mankind lives.

IV
Resolution on the Recent Disturbances

The Working Committee of the Indian National Congress are of opinion that the recent distrubances created by the people in Bombay, Delhi, Calcutta and other places were in every way harmful and were an obstacle in the way of the Congress. These included arson and incendiarism whether of private shops or public places, looting, especially destruction of foodstuffs, frightening pedestrians, compelling people to shout slogans, compelling Europeans to remove their hats and otherwise molesting them. All these acts were manifestly against the policy of non-violence adopted by the Congresss and were derogatory to national dignity. Whilst there is nothing but unmixed condemnation of popular frenzy, this Committee, without prejuding the military action taken in order to deal with the recent outburst of violence, are of opinion that the popular belief, generally and justly, has been that such action has been taken in excess of necessity and in order to strike terror in the hearts of the people and that therefore the military have bulleted passers-by or even innocent people, men, women or children standing in thier own galleries. Any such action, at the present moment, instead of cowing down the populace, has the effect of infuriating it. The Committee, therefore, ask the Government to institute and inquiry into the military action taken in the various places and hope that the inquiry will be open and public and will have on it representatives with judicial qualifications and enjoying public confidence. At the same time the Committee hope that the people will observe restraint befitting the Congress and help the conference between the Cabinet Mission and the representatives of the people to carry on their work in a calm atmosphere.

Document No. 91

LETTER FROM SADIQ ALI TO MAULANA AZAD

March 26, 1946

Dear Maulana Sahib,

I am quoting below a telegram we have received from Mombasa.

MOMBASA
INDIAN NATIONAL CONGRESS ALLAHABAD

FOOD FOR INDIA CAMPAIGN LAUNCHED IN EAST AFRICA STOP KINDLY ADVISE BEST FORM ASSISTANCE WE CAN RENDER AND SUGGEST CENTRAL RELIEF ORGANIZATION CONCERNED

CONGRESS

Please let us know if you want us to send any reply to this telegram. I have sent a copy of the telegram to Gandhiji.

Yours sincerely,
Sadiq Ali

Maulana Abul Kalam Azad,
President A.I.C.C.,
Calcutta

Document No. 92

PAKISTAN AGAINST MUSLIMS' INTERESTS[1]

As is well-known, Mr. Jinnah's Pakistan scheme is based on his two-nation theory. His thesis is that India contains many nationalities based on religious differences. Of them the two major nations, the Hindus and Muslims, must as separate nations have separate states. When Dr. Edward Thompson once pointed out to Mr. Jinnah that Hindus and Muslims live side by side in thousands of Indian towns, villages and hamlets, Mr. Jinnah replied that this in no way affected their separate nationality. Two nations, according to Mr. Jinnah, confront one another in every hamlet, village and town, and he therefore, desires that they should be separated into two states.

I am prepared to overlook all other aspects of the problem and judge it from the point of view of Muslim interests alone. I shall go still further and say that if it can be shown that the scheme of Pakistan can in any way benefit Muslims as such, I would be prepared to accept it myself and also to work for its acceptance by others. But the truth is that even if I examine the scheme from the point of view of the communal interests of the Muslims themselves, I am forced to the conclusion that it can in no way benefit them or allay their legitimate fears.

Let us consider dispassionately the consequence which will follow if we give effect to the Pakistan scheme. India will be divided into two States, one with a majority of Muslims and the other of Hindus. In the Hindustan State there will remain three-and-a-half crore Muslims scattered in small minorities all over the land. With 17 per cent in U.P. 12 per cent in Bihar and 9 per cent in Madras, they will be weaker than they are today in the Hindu majority provinces. They have had their homelands in these regions for almost a thousand years and built up most well-known centres of Muslim culture and civilization there.

They will awaken overnight and discover that hey have become aliens and foreigners, backward industrially, edcucationally and economically; they will be left to the mercies of what would become an unadulterated Hindu Raj.

On the other hand, their position within the Pakistan State will be vulnerable and weak. Nowhere in Pakistan will their majority be comparable to the Hindu majority in the Hindustan State. In fact, their majority will be so slight that it will be offset by the economical, educational and political lead enjoyed by non-Muslims in these areas. Even if this were not so and Pakistan were overwhelmingly Muslim in population, it still could hardly solve the problem of Muslims in Hindustan. Two states confronting one another offer no solution to the problems of one another's minorities, but only lead to retribution and reprisals by introducing a system of mutual hostages. The scheme of Pakistan, therefore, solves no problems for the Muslims. It cannot safeguard their rights where they are in a minority, nor as citizens of Pakistan secure them a position in India or world affairs which they would enjoy as citizens of a major State like the Indian Union.

It may be argued that if Pakistan is so much against the interests of the Muslims themselves, why should such a large section of Muslims be swept away by its lure? The answer is to be found in the attitude of certain communal extremists among the Hindus. When the Muslim League began to speak of Pakistan, they read into the scheme a sinister pan-Islamic conspiracy and began to oppose it out of fear that it foreshadowed a combination of Indian Muslims with trans-Indian Muslim States. This opposition acted as an incentive to the adherents of the League. With simple though untenable logic, they argued that if Hindus were so opposed to Pakistan, surely, it must be of benefit to Muslims. An atmosphere of emotional frenzy was created which made reasonable appraisement impossible and swept away especially the younger and more impressionable among the Muslims. I have, however, no doubt that when the present frenzy has died down and the question can be considered dispassionately, those who now support Pakistan will themselves repudiate it as harmful for Muslim interests.

The formula which I have succeeded in making the Congress accept secures whatever merit the Pakistan scheme contains, while all its defects and drawbacks are avoided. The basis of Pakistan is the fear of interference by the Centre majority areas, as the Hindus will be in a majority in the Centre. The Congress meets this fear by granting full autonomy to the provincial units and vesting all residuary power in the provinces. It also has provided for two lists of Central subjects, one compulsory and one optional, so that if any provincial unit so desires it can administer all subjects itself except a minimum delegated to the Centre. The Congress scheme, therefore, ensures that Muslim majority provinces are internally free to develop as they will, but can, at the same time influence the Centre on all issues which affect India as a whole.

The situation in India is such that all attempts to establish a centralized and unitary government are bound to fail. Equally doomed to failure is the attempt to divide India into two states. After considering all aspects of the questions, I have come to the conclusion that the only solution can be on lines embodied in the Congress formula which allows room for development both to the provinces and to India as a whole. The Congress formula meets the fears of the Muslim majority areas to allay which the scheme of Pakistan was formed; on the other hand, it avoids the defects of the Pakistan scheme which would bring the Muslims where they are in a minority under a purely Hindu Government.

I am one of those who consider the present document of communal bitterness and differences a transient phase in Indian life. It firmly holds that they will disappear when India assumes the responsibility for her own destiny. I am reminded of a saying of Mr. Gladstone that the best cure for a man's fear of the water was to throw him into it, for he would then learn to swim and realize that it is not so dangerous as it had seemed to his imagination. Similarly, India must assume responsibility and administer her own affairs. When India attains her destiny, she will forget the present document of communal suspicion and conflict and face the problems of modern life from a modern point of view.

Differences will no doubt persist, but they will be economic not communal. Opposition among political parties will continue but it will be based not on religion but on economic and political issues. Class and not community will be the basis of future alignments and policies will be shaped accordingly. If it be argued that this is only a faith which events may not justify, I would say that in any case the nine crores of Muslims constitute a factor which nobody can ignore, and, whatever the circumstances, they are strong enough to safeguard their own destiny.

---

1. Statement of Maulana Azad dated 17.4.1946.

Document No. 93

LETTER FROM PATHICK LAWRENCE TO MAULANA AZAD

NEW DELHI
27.4.1946

Dear Maulana Saheb,

The Cabinet Mission and His Excellency the viceroy have come to the conclusion that they should make one further attempt to obtain agreement between the Muslim League and the Congress. They realize that it wold be useless to ask the two parties to meet, unless they were able to place before them a basis of negotiation, which could lead to such an agreement.

I am, therefore, asked to invite the Muslim League to send four negotiators to meet the Cabinet Mission and the Viceroy, together with a similar number from the Congress Working Committee, with a view to discussing the possibility of agreement upon a scheme based upon the following fundamental principles.

The future constitutional structure of the British India to be as follows :

A Union Government leading with the following subjects –

The Foreign Affairs, and

Defence and Communications

There will be two groups of provinces, the one of the predominantly Hindu provinces and the other of the predominantly Muslim provinces, dealing with all other subjects which the provinces in the respective groups desire to be dealt with in common. The provincial governments will deal with all other subjects and they will have at the residuary sovereign rights.

It is contemplated that the Indian states will take their appropriate place in this structure on terms to be negotiated with them.

Yours sincerely,
Pathick Lawrence

Document No. 94

LETTER FROM MAULANA AZAD TO PATHICK LAWRENCE

20, Akbar Road,
New Delhi
28th April, 1946

My dear Lord Pathick Lawrence,

I thank you for your letter of April 27th. I have consulted my Colleagues of the Congress Working Committee in regard to the suggestion made by you, and they desire me to inform you that they have always been willing to discuss fully any matters concerning the future of India with representatives of the Muslim League or any other organization. I must point out, however, that the "Fundamental Principles" which you mention require amplification and elucidation in order to avoid any misunderstanding.

As you are aware, we have envisaged a Federal Union of autonomous units. Such a Federal Union must of necessity deal with certain essential subject of which defence and its allied subjects are the most important. It must be organic and must have both an executing and legislative machinery as well as the finance relating to those subjects and the power to raise revenues for these purposes in its own right. Without these functions and powers it would be weak and defence and progress in general would suffer. Thus among the common subjects in addition to Foreign Affairs, Defence and Communications, there should be Currency. Customs and such other subjects as may be found on close scrutiny to be ultimately allied to them.

Your reference to two groups of provinces, the one of the predominantly Hindu provinces and the other of the predominantly Muslim provinces, is not clear. The only predominantly Muslim Provinces are the North-West Frontier Province, Sind and Baluchistan. Bengal and Punjab have a bore Muslim Majority. We consider it wrong to form groups of provinces under the Federal Union and more so on religious or communal basis. It also appears that you have no choice to a province in the matter of joining or not joining a group. It is by no means certain that a province is constituted would like to join any particular group. In any event it would be wholly wrong to compel a province to function against its own wish. While we agree to the provinces having full powers in regard to all remaining subjects as well as the residuary power. We have also stated that it should be open to any province to exercise its option to have more common subjects with the federal union. Any sub-Federation within the Federal Union would weaken the Federal Centre and would be otherwise wrong. We do not, therefore, favour any such development.

Regarding the Indian states we should like to make it clear that we consider it essential that they should be parts of the Federal Union in regard to the common subjects mentioned above. The manner of their coming into the Union can be considered fully later.

You have referred to certain "Fundamental Principles" but there is no mention of the basic issue before us, that is, Indian independence and the consequent withdrawal of the British army from India. It is only on this basis that we can discuss the future of India or any interim arrangement.

While we can ready to carry on negotiations with any party as to the future of India, We must state our conviction that reality will be absent from any negotiations whilst an outside ruling power still exists in India.

I have asked three of my colleagues of the Congress Working Committee, namely Pandit Jawaharlal Nehru, Sardar Vallabhbhai Patel and Khan Abdul Gaffar Khan to accompany me in any negotiations that may take place as the result of your suggestion.

Yours sincerely,
Abul Kalam Azad

Lord Pathick Lawrence,
New Delhi

Document No. 95

LETTER FROM LAWRENCE TO MAULANA AZAD

New Delhi,
29th April, 1946

Dear Maulana Saheb,

Thank you for your letter of 28th April. The Cabinet Delegation are very glad to know that the Congress agree to enter the joint discussion with representatives of the Muslim League and ourselves.

We have taken note of the views you have expressed on behalf of the Working Committee of Congress. These appear to deal with matters which can be discussed at the Conference for we have never completed that acceptance by Congress and the Muslim League of such invitation would imply as a preliminary condition full approval by them or the terms set out in my letter. These terms are our proposed basis for a settlement and what we have asked the Congress Working Committee to do is regret to send its representatives to meet ourselves and representatives of the Muslim League in order to discuss it.

Assuming that the Muslim League, whose reply we expect to receive in the course of the afternoon also accept our invitation, we propose that these discussions, should be held at Simla, and intend to move there ourselves on Wednesday next, we hope that you will be able to arrange for the Congress representatives to be in Simla in time to open the discussion on the morning of Thursday, May 2nd.

Yours sincerely,
Pathick Lawrence

Maulana Abul Kalam Azad,
President I.N.C.,
New Delhi

Document No. 96

LETTER FROM MAULANA AZAD TO PATHICK LAWRENCE

New Delhi,
6th May, 1946

Dear Lord Pathick Lawrence,

My Colleagues and I followed with care the proceedings of the Conference yesterday and tried to understand what our conversations were leading up to. I confess to feeling somewhat mystified and disturbed at the vagueness of our talks and some of the assumptions underlying them while we would like to associate ourselves with every effort to explore ways and means of finding a basis for agreement, we must not deceive ourselves, the Cabinet Mission or the representatives of the Muslim League into the belief that the way the Conference has so far proceeded furnishes hope of success. Our general approach to the question before us was stated briefly in my letter to you of April 28th. We find that this approach has been largely ignored and a contrary method has been followed. We realise that some assumptions have to be made in the early stages as otherwise there can be no progress. But assumptions which ignore or run contrary to fundamental issues are likely to lead to misunderstanding during the later stages.

In my letter of April 28th I stated that the basic issue before us was that of Indian Independence and the consequent withdrawal of the British army from India, for there can be no independence so long as there is a foreign army on Indian soil. We stand for the independence of the whole of India now and not in the distant or near future. Other matters are subsidiary to this and can be petty discussed and decided by the Constituent Assembly.

At the Conference yesterday I refered to this again and we were glad to find that you and your colleagues, as well as the other members of the Conference, accepted Indian independence as the basis of our talks. It was stated by you that the Constituent Assembly would finally decide about the independence of or other relationship that might be established between a free India and England. While this is perfectly true, it does not effect the position now, and that is the acceptance of Indian Independence now.

If that is so then certain consequences inevitably follow. We felt yesterday that there was no appreciation of these consequences. A Constituent Assembly is not going to decide the question of independence that question must be and, we take it, has been decided now. That Assembly will represent the will of the free Indian Nation and give effect to it. It is not going to be bound by any previous arrangements. It has to be preceded by a Provisional Government which should undertake to make all arrangements for the transitional period.

In our discussion yesterday repeated references were made to 'groups' of provinces functioning together, and it was even suggested that such a group would have an executive and legislative machinery. This method of grouping has not so far been discussed by us but still our talks seemed to presume all this. I should like to make it very clear that we are entirely...opposed to any executive or legislative machinery for a group of provinces or units of the Federation. That will mean a sub-federation, if not something more, and we have already told you that we do not accept this. It would result in creating three layers of executive and legislative bodies, an arrangement which will be combrous, static and disjointed, leading to continuous friction. We are not aware of any such arrangement in any country.

We are emphatically of opinion that it is not open to the Conference to entertain any suggestions for a division of India. If this to come, it should come through the Constituent Assembly free from any influence of the present governing power.

Another point we wish to make clear is that we do not accept the proposal for parity as between groups in regard to the executive or legislative. We realise that everything possible should be done to remove fears and suspicions from the mind of every group and community. But the way to do this is not by unreal methods which go against the basic principles of democracy on which we hope to build up our constitution.

Yours sincerely,
A.K. Azad

Lord Pathick Lawrence (O.C.D.),
Viceroy's House,
New Delhi

Document No. 97

LETTER FROM THE P.S. TO LORD LAWRENCE TO MAULANA AZAD

Office of the Cabinet Mission Delegation,
The Viceroy's House,
New Delhi,
8th May, 1946

Dear Sir,

With reference to the Secretary of State's letter to you this morning the Cabinet Delegation wish me to send you the enclosed document which is the paper to which the Secretary of State referred. The Delegation propose that this paper should be discussed at the next meeting to be held on Thursday afternoon at 3 P.M. if, that is agreeable to the Congress/Muslim League delegates.

Yours sincerely,
Private Secretary to Lord Pathick Lawrence

Copy to :
Maulana Abul Kalam Azad,
President, Indian National Congress

Encl : 1-

Enclosure

1. There shall be an All India Union Government and Legislative dealing with Foreign Affairs, Defence, Communications, Fundamental rights and having the necessary Powers to obtain for itself the Finances it requires for these subjects.
2. All the remaining powers shall vest in the Provinces.
3. Groups of Provinces may be formed and such groups may determine the Provincial subjects which they desire to take in common.

4. The groups may set up their own executives and Legislatures.
5. The legislature of the Union shall be composed of equal proportions from the Muslim-majority Provinces and from the Hindu-majority Provinces whether or not these or any of them have formed themselves into groups together with representatives of the states.
6. The Government of the Union shall be constituted in the same proportion as the legislature.
7. The Constitution of the Union and the groups (if any) shall contain a provision whereby any province can be a majority vote of its Legislative Assembly call for a reconsideration of the terms of the constitution after an initial period of 10 years and at 10 yearly intervals thereafter.

For the purpose of such reconsideration a body shall be constituted on the same basis as the original Constituent Assembly and with the same provisions as to voting and shall have power to amend the constitution in any way decided upon.

8. The Constitution making machinery to arrive at a constitution on the above basis shall be as follows:
   A. Representatives shall be elected from each provincial Assembly in proportion to the strengths of the various parties in that Assembly on the basis of 1/10 of their numbers.
   B. Representatives shall be invited from the states on the basis of their population in proportion to the representation from British India.
   C. The Constituent Assembly so formed shall meet at earliest date possible in New Delhi.
   D. After its preliminary meeting at which the general order of business will be settled it will divide into three sections. One Section ...representing the Hindu-majority Provinces, one section representing the Muslim-majority Provinces and are representing the states.
   E. The first two sections will then meet separately to decide the Provincial Constitution for their group and, if they wish, a group constitution.
   F. When these have settled it will be open to any province to decide to opt out of its original group and into the other group or to remain outside any group.
   G. Thereafter the three bodies will meet together to settle the Constitution for the Union on the lines agreed in paragraphs 1 to 7 above.

H. No major point in the Union Constitution which effects the communal issue shall be deemed to be passed by the Assembly unless a majority of both thė two major communities vote in its favour.

I. The Viceroy shall forthwith call together the above Constitution making machinery which shall be governed by the provisions stated in paragraph 8 above.

Document No. 98

LETTER FROM MAULANA AZAD TO PATHICK LAWRENCE

New Delhi,
9th May, 1946

Dear Lord Lawrence,

My Colleagues and I have given the most careful consideration to the memorandum sent by you yesterday suggesting various points of agreement. On the 28th April I sent you a letter in which I explained briefly the Congress viewpoint in regard to certain 'Fundamental Principles' mentioned in your letter of 27th April. After the first day of Conference on May 6th, I wrote to you again to avoid any possible misunderstanding regarding the issues being discussed in the conference.

I now find from your memorandum that some of your suggestions are opposed to our view and to the views repeatedly declared by the Congress. We are thus placed in a difficult position. It has been and is our desire to explore every avenue for a settlement and a change over in India by consent, and for this purpose, we are prepared to go for. But there are obvious limits beyond which we cannot go and we are convinced that this would be injurious to the people of India and to India's progress as a free nation.

In my previous letter I have paid stress on the necessity of having a strong and organic Federal Union. I have also stated that we do not approve of sub-federations or grouping of Provinces in the manner suggested and are wholly opposed to parity in executive or legislatures as between wholly unequal groups we do not wish to come in way of provinces of other units co-operating together.

The proposals you have put forward are meant, we presume, to limit the free discretion of the Constituent Assembly. We do not see how this can be done. We are at present concerned with one important aspect of a larger problem. Any decision on this aspect taken now might well conflict with ... the decision we, or the Constituent Assembly, might want to take on other aspects. The only reasonable course appears to us is to have a Constituent Assembly with perfect freedom to draw up its constitution, with certain reservations to protect the rights of minorities. Thus we may agree that any major communal issue must be settled by consent of the perfect concerned or, where such consent is not obtained, by arbitration.

From the proposals you have sent us (8 O.E.F.G.) it would appear that two or three separate constitutions might emerge for separate groups, joined together by a flimsy common superstructure left to the mercy of the three disjointed groups.

There is also compulsion in the early stages for a province to join a particular group whether it wants or not. Thus why should the Frontier Province, which is clearly a Congress Province, be compelled to join any group hostile to the Congress?

We realise that in dealing with human beings, as individuals or groups many considerations have to be borne in mind besides logic and reason. But logic and reason cannot be ignored altogether, and unreason and injustice are dangerous companions at any time, and more especially, when we are building for the future of hundreds of millions of human beings.

I shall now deal with some of the points in your memorandum and make some suggestions in regard to them.

No. 1. We note that you have provided for the union to have necessary powers to obtain for itself the finance it requires for the subject it deals with. We think it should be clearly stated that the Federal Union must have power to raise revenues in its own right. Further that currency and customs must in any event be included in the union subjects, as well as such other subjects as on closer scrutiny may be found to be intimately allied to them one other subject is an essential and inevitable Union subject and that is planning. Planning can only be done effectively at the Centre, though the Provinces or units will give effect to it in their respective areas.

The Union must also have power to take remedial action in cases of breakdown of the constitution and in grave public emergencies.

Nos. 5 and 6. We are entirely opposed to the proposed parity, both in the Executive and Legislature, as between wholly unequal groups. This is unfair and will lead to trouble. Such a provision contains in itself the seed of conflicts and the destruction of free growth. If there is no agreement on this or any similar matter we are prepared to leave it to arbitration.

No. 7. We are prepared to accept the suggestion that provision be made for a reconsideration of the constitution after ten years.

Indeed the constitution will necessarily provide the machinery for ...its revision at any time.

The second clause lays down that reconsideration should be done by a body constituted on the same basis as the Constituent Assembly. This present provision is intended to meet an emergency. We expect that the Constitution for India will be based on adult suffrage. Ten years hence, India is not likely to be satisfied with anything less than adult suffrage to express its mind on all grave issues.

No. 8A. We would suggest that the jsut and proper recommendation for constitution, fail to all parties, is the method of proportional representation by single transferable vote. It might be remembered that the present basis of election for the Provincial Assemblies is strongly weighted in favour of the minorities.

The proportion of 1/10th appears to be too small and will limit the numbers of the Constituent Assembly too much. Probably the number would not exceed 200. In the vitally important talks the Assembly will have to face, it should have larger numbers. We suggest that at least one fifth of the total membership of the provincial Assemblies should be elected for the Constituent Assembly.

No. 8B. This clause is vague and requires elucidation. But for the present we are not going into further details.

No. 8DEFG. I have already referred to these clauses. We think that both the formation of these groups and the procedure suggested (that) are wrong and undesirable. We do not wish to rule out the formation of the groups if the provinces so desire. But this subject must be left open for decision by the Constituent Assembly. The drafting and the setting of the constitution should begin with the Federal Union. This should contain common and uniform provisions for the provinces and other units. The provinces may then add to these.

No. 8H. In the circumstances existing today we are prepared to accept some such clauses. In case of disagreement the matter should be referred to arbitration.

I have pointed out above some of the obvious defects, as we see them, in the proposals contained in your memorandum. If these are remedied, as suggested by us, we might be in a position to recommend their acceptance by the Congress. But as drafted in the memorandum sent to us. I regret that we are unable to accept them.

On the whole, therefore, if the suggestions are intended to have a binding effect, with all the will in the world to have an agreement with the League, we must repudiate most of them. Let us not run into any evil greater than the one all to us three parties should seek to avoid.

If an agreement honourable to both the parties and favourable to the growth of free and united India cannot be achieved, we would suggest that an Interim Provisional Government responsible to the elected members of the Central Assembly be formed at once and the matters in dispute concerning the Constituent Assembly between the Congress and the League be referred to an independent tribunal.

Yours sincerely,
A.K. Azad

Lord Pathick Lawrence,
New Delhi

Document No. 99

LETTER FROM MAULANA AZAD TO LORD LAWRENCE

20, Akbar Road,
New Delhi,

20th May, 1946

Dear Lord Pathick Lawrence,

My Committee have carefully considered the statement issued by the Cabinet Delegation on May 16th, and they have seen Gandhiji after the interviews he has had with you and Sir Stafford Cripps. There are certain matters about which I have been asked to write to you.

As we understand the statement, it contains certain recommendations and procedure for the election and functioning of the Constituent Assembly. The Assembly itself, when proved, will in my Committee's opinion, be a sovereign body for the purpose of drafting the constitution unkindered by any external authority, as well as for entering into a treaty. Further that it will be open to the Assembly to vary in any way it likes the recommendations and the procedure suggested by the Cabinet Delegation. The Constituent Assembly being a sovereign body for the purpose of the constitution its final decision will automatically take effect.

As you were aware some recommendations have been made in your statement which are contrary to the Congress stand as it was taken at the Simla Conference and elsewhere. Naturally we shall try to get the Assembly to remove what we consider defects in the recommendations. For this purpose we shall endeavour to educate the country and the Constituent Assembly.

This is one matter in which my Committee were pleased to hear Gandhiji say that you were trying to see that the European members in the various provincial assemblies, particularly Bengal and Assam would neither offer themselves as candidates nor vote for the election of delegates to the Constituent Assembly.

No provision has been made for the election of a representative from British Baluchistan. So far as we know, there is no elected

Assembly or any other kind of chamber which might select such a representative. One individual may not make much of a difference in the Constituent Assembly, but it would make a difference if such an individual speaks for a whole province which he really does not represent in any way. It is far better not to have representation at all than to have this kind of representation which will mislead and which may decide the fact of Baluchistan contrary to the wishes of its inhabitants. If any kind of popular representation can be arranged we would welcome it. My Committee were pleased, therefore, to hear Gandhiji say that you are likely to include Baluchistan within the scope of Advisory Committee's work.

In your recommendations for the basic form of the constitution you state that provinces should be free to form groups with executives and legislatives and each group could determine the provincial subjects to be taken in common. Just previous to this you state all subjects other than the union subjects and all residuary powers should vest in the provinces. Later on in the statement, however, you state that "the provincial representatives to the Constituent Assembly will divide up into three sections and these sections shall proceed to settle the provincial constitutions for the provinces in each section and also decide whether any group constitution shall be set up for these provinces." There appears to us to be a marked discrepancy in these two separate provinces. The basic provision gives full autonomy to a province to do what it likes and subsequently there appears to be a certain compulsion in the matter which clearly infringes that autonomy. It is true that at a later state the provinces can opt out of any group. In any event it is not clear how a province or its representatives can be compelled to do something which they do not want to do. A Provincial Assembly may give a mandate to its representatives not to enter any group or a particular group or section. As Sections B and C have been formed it is obvious that one province will play a dominating role in the section, the Punjab in Section B and Bengal in Section C. It is conceivable that this dominating province may frame a provincial constitution entirely against the wishes of Sind or the North-West Frontier Province or Assam. It may even conceivable lay down rules, for elections and otherwise thereby nullifying the Provision for a province to opt out of a group. Such could never be the intention as it would be repugnant to the basic principles and policy of the Scheme itself.

The question of the Indian states has been left vague and, therefore, I need not say much about at this stage. But it is clear that state representatives who come into the Constituent Assembly must do so more or less in the same way as the representatives of the provinces. The Constituent Assembly cannot be formed of entirely desparate elements.

I have dealt above with some points arising out of your statement possibly some of them can be cleared up by you and the defects removed. The Principal point, however, is, as stated above, that we lean upon this Constituent Assembly as a sovereign body which can decide as it chooses in regard to my matter before it can give effect to its decision. The only limitation we recognise is that in regard to certain major communal issues the decision should be by a majority of each of the two major communities. We shall try to approach the public and the members of the Constituent Assembly with our own proposals for removing any defects in the recommendations made by you.

Gandhiji has informed my Committees that you contemplate that British troops will remain in India till after the establishment of the Government in accordance with the instrument produced by the Constituent Assembly. My Committee feel that the presence of foreign troops in India will be a negation of India's independence. India should be considered to be independent in fact from the moment that the National Provisional Government is established.

I shall be grateful to have an early reply so that my Committee may come to a decision in regard to your statement.

Yours sincerely,
Abul Kalam Azad

The Rt. Hon'ble Lord Pathick Lawrence,
Office of the Cabinet Delegation,
Viceroy's House,
New Delhi

Document No. 100

NATIONAL LANGUAGE OF INDIA

By Maulana Azad

21-5-1946

Gandhiji has given many things to India, but probably very few people realize that one of the biggest things that she has received at his hands is the idea of national language. Although she could boast of several languages there was none which was universally accepted as her national language.

English came to us through the Government, but soon it so dominated the country that it became the medium for higher education and social inter-course among the educated class. They were ashamed to speak in their national language and considered it a mark of honour and distinction to speak in English only on all occasions. Even in their private conversations they could not put away their English.

A new political awakening came over the country towards the close of the last century when the Indian National Congress was founded. The sessions of the Congress were held to make the demands and decisions of the nation heard to the world. But even this voice was not in the national tongue. We wanted to proclaim to England that India was for Indians and for none other. But to say that, we could find no language of our own and were content to express our longing in a borrowed tongue.

The entry of Gandhiji in the political field spelt a complete revolution– the country began to speak in its own tongues. To speak in the national tongue ceased to be regarded as a shame. Gandhiji reminded the people that the thing to be ashamed of was to forget one's own tongue. He toured all over the country in 1920-21 and delivered hundreds of speeches but without exception they were in Hindustani.

When I was under detention at Ranchi during the Great War, I remember having read in the newspapers the report of the War Conference which Lord Chelmsford had summoned in 1917. Gandhiji participated in it, but he had made it a condition that he would speak in Hindustani. At that time this was regarded by the Press as a strange innovation. But the innovation was soon to become the common thing in the country and today we see that Hindustani has taken the place that English held twenty-five years ago.

Document No. 101

LETTER FROM PATHICK LAWRENCE TO MAULANA AZAD

Office of the Cabinet Delegation,
Viceroy's House,
New Delhi,

22nd May, 1946

Dear Maulana Saheb,

The delegation have considered your letter of 20th May and feel that the best way to answer it is that they should make their general position quite clear to you. Since the Indian leaders after prolonged discussion failed to arrive at an agreement the Delegation have put forward their recommendations as the nearest approach to reconciling the views of the two main parties. The scheme therefore stands as a whole and can only succeed if it is accepted and worked in a spirit of compromise on cooperation.

You are aware of the reasons for the grouping of the provinces, and this is an essential feature for the scheme which can only be modified by agreement between the two parties.

There are two further points which we think we should mention. First, in your letter you described the Constituent Assembly as a sovereign body, the final decision of which will automatically take effect. We think the authority and the functions of the Constituent Assembly and the procedure which it is intended to follow are clear from the statement. Once the Constituent Assembly is formed and working on this basis, there is naturally no intention to interfere with its discretion or to question its decision. When the Constituent Assembly has completed its labours. His Majesty's Government will recommend to Parliament such action as may be necessary for the cession of sovereignty to the Indian People, Subject only to two provisions which are mentioned in the statement and which are not, we believe controversial, namely, adequate provision for the protection of minorities and willingness to conclude a treaty to cover matters arising out of the transfer of power.

Secondly, while His Majesty's Government are most anxious to secure that the interim period should be as short as possible, you will, we are sure, appreciate, that for the reason stated above, independence cannot precede the bringing into operation a new constitution.

Yours sincerely,
Pathick Lawrence

Maulan Abul Kalam Azad,
New Delhi

Document No. 102

LETTER FROM MAULANA AZAD TO LORD WAVELL

20, Akbar Road,
New Delhi,
May 25, 1946

Dear Lord Wavell,

Your Excellency will remember that the demand of the Congress from the very beginning of the present discussion regarding the Interim Government has been that there must be a legal and constitutional change in order to give it the status of a truly national government. The Working Committee has felt that this is necessary in the interest of a peaceful settlement of the Indian Problem. Without such status the Interim Government would not be in a position to infuse in the Indian people a consciousness of freedom which is today essential. Both Lord Pathick Lawrence and you have, however pointed out the difficulties in the way of effecting such constitutional changes, while at the same time assuring as that the Interim Government would have in fact, if not in law, the status of a truly national government. The Working Committee feel that after the British Government's declaration that the Constituent Assembly will be the final authority for passing the constitution and any constitution framed by it will be binding, the recognition of Indian independence is imminent. It is inevitable that the Interim Government which is to function during the period of the Constituent Assembly must reflect this recognition. In my last conversation with you, you stated that it was your intention to function as a constitution head of the Government and that in practice the Interim Government would have the same power as that of a Cabinet in the Dominions. This is, however, a matter which is so important that it would not be fair either to you or to the Congress Working Committee to let it rest upon what transpired in informal conversations. Even without any change in the law there could be some formal understanding by which the Congress Working Committee may be assured that the Interim Government would in practice function like a dominion Cabinet.

The question of the responsibility of the Interim Government to the Central Assembly may also be treated in the same way. The existing law permits an executive independence of the Central Legislature but a convention could be created by which its tenure of office would depend on its enjoyment of such confidence.

The other details regarding the composition and magnitude of the Interim Cabinet which came up in my discussion with you would all depend upon the satisfactory solution of the two basic questions enumerated above. If the question of status and responsibility of the Interim Government is satisfactorily solved I hope we would be able to decide other questions without any delay. I have already written to you, the Working Committee has been adjourned and will be summoned again when occasion demands. I would request you to let me have an indication of your decision and programme so that the Working Committee may be summoned accordingly. I am leaving for Massorie on Monday and would request you to reply to my letter there.

Yours sincerely,
A.K. Azad

H.E. Field Marshall Viscount Wavell,
The Viceroy's House,
New Delhi

Document No. 103

LETTER FROM LORD WAVELL TO MAULANA AZAD

The Viceroy's House,
New Delhi,

30th May, 1946.

My dear Maulana Saheb,

1. I have received your letter of the 25th May on the Interim Government.

2. We have discussed this matter on several occasions and I recognise the importance that you and your party attach to a satisfactory definition of the Powers of the Interim Government and appreciate your reasons for asking for such a definitions. My difficulty is that the most liberal intentions may be almost unrecognisable when they have to be expressed in a formal document.

3. I am quite clear that I did not state to you that the Interim government would have the same powers as a Dominion Cabinet. The whole constitutional polity is entirely different. I said that I was sure that His Majesty's Government would treat the new Interim Government with the same consultation and consideration as a Dominion Government.

4. His Majesty's Government have already said that they will give to the Indian government the greatest possible freedom in the exercised of the day today administration of the country; and I need hardly assure you that it is my intention faithfully to carry out this undertaking.

5. I am quite clear that the spirit in which the government is worked will be of much greater importance than any formal document and guarantee. I have no doubt that if you are prepared to trust me, we shall be able to co-operate in a manner which will give India a sense of freedom from external control and will prepare for complete freedom as soon as the new constitution is made.

6. I sincerely hope that the Congress will accept these assurances and will have no further hesitation in going to co-operate in the immense problems which control us.

7. In the matter of time-table you will be aware that the All India Muslim League Council is meeting on June 5th at which we understand decisive conclusions are to be reached. I suggest, therefore, that if you summon your Working Committee to reassemble in Delhi on Friday, the 7th, it may be possible for final discussions to be made by all parties on outstanding questions early in the following week.

Yours sincerely,
Wavell

Maulana Abul Kalam Azad,
New Delhi

Document No. 104

LETTER FROM MAULANA AZAD TO LORD WAVELL

20, Akbar Road,
New Delhi,
13th June, 1946

Dear Lord Wavell,

Thank you for your letter of the 12th June, which I have just received, inquiring after my health. I have now more or less recovered.

Pandit Jawaharlal Nehru has reported to my Committee and me the gist of the conversation between your excellency and him. My committee regret that they are unable to accept your suggestions for the formation of the Provisional National Government. These tentative suggestions emphasise the principle of 'Parity' to which we have been and are entirely opposed. In composition of the Cabinet suggested by you there is 'Parity' between the Hindus including the Scheduled Castes and the Muslim League, that is the number of Caste Hindus is actually less than the nominees of the Muslim League. The position thus is worse than it was in June 1945 at Simla where, according to your declaration then, there was to be 'Parity' between Caste Hindus and Muslims, leaving additional seats for the Scheduled Caste Hindus. The Muslim seats then were not reserved for the Muslim League only but could include non-League Muslims. The present proposal thus puts the Hindus in a very unfair position and at the same time eliminate the non-League Muslims. My Committee are not prepared to accept any proposal Indeed as we have stated repeatedly we are opposed to 'Parity' in any step of form.

In addition to this 'Parity' we are told that there should be a convention requiring that major communal issues should be decided by separate group voting. While we have accepted this principle for long-term arrangements we did so as an effective substitute for other safeguards. In your present proposal, however, both 'Parity' and this convention are suggested. This would make the working of the Provisional Government almost impossible and deadlock a certainty.

As I have often pointed out to you we are strongly of opinion that the Provisional Government should consist of fifteen members. This is necessary to carry out the administration of the country efficiently as well as to give adequate representation to the smaller minorities. We are anxious that the various minorities should have scope in such a Government. The work before the Provisional Government is likely to be much heavier and more exacting. In your proposals communications include railways, transport, telegraphs and air. It is difficult for us to conceive how all these can be joined together in one portfolio. This would be highly undesirable at any time. With industrial troubles and the possibility of railways strikes this arrangement would be wholly wrong. We think also that the planning is an essential department, therefore, the provisional government must consist of fifteen members.

The suggested division of portfolios appears to us to be undesirable and unfair.

My Committee would also like to point out that a coalition government in order to be successful must have some common outlook and programme for the time being. The manner of approach in forming such a government has been such as to leave this ...out of consideration and my Committee do not feel any confidence that such a coalition can function successfully.

It was our intention to write to you about certain other matters also, but for reasons known to you our letter has been delayed. I shall write to you about these other matters later. My purpose in writing to you is not to convey to you without any delay our reaction on the tentative proposals that you put forward today.

Yours sincerely,
A.K. Azad

His Excellency,
Field-Marshal Viscocent Wavell,
Viceroy's House,
New Delhi

Document No. 105

LETTER FROM MAULANA AZAD TO LORD WAVELL

20, Akbar Road,
New Delhi,

14th June, 1946

Dear Lord Wavell,

In my letter to you sent yesterday I promised to send you another letter. I am now doing so.

On May 24th the Congress Working Committee passed a resolution which I conveyed to you. In this resolution we have our reaction to the statement dated May 16, 1946, which the British Cabinet Delegation and you issued on behalf of the British Government. We pointed out what were in our opinion some of the omissions and defects in that statement and we also gave our interpretation of some of its provisions. In a subsequent statement issued by you and the Cabinet Delegation our viewpoint was not accepted.

You know, and we have repeatedly emphasised this, that our immediate objective has been and is the independence of India. We have to judge everything by this standard. We suggested that even though no legal change might be made at this stage, independence in practice might be recognised. This has not been agreed to.

In your letter dated May 30, 1946, addressed to me, you explained what in your view (that) the status and powers of the Interim Government would be. This too falls short of what we aim it. Yet the friendly tone of your letter and our desire to find some way out led us to accept your assurance in these matters. We came to the conclusion also that, unsatisfactory as were many of the provisions of your statement of May 16th, we would try to work them according to our own interpretation and with a view to achieve our objective.

You are no doubt aware of the strong feeling of resentment which exists among long sections of the people against some of the proposals in the statement, notably the idea of grouping. The Frontier Province and Assam have pressed themselves with considerable force against any compulsory grouping. The Sikhs have felt hurt and isolated by these proposals and are considerably agitated. Being a minority in the Punjab, they become still more helpless, as far as numbers go, in Section 'B' we appreciated all these objections especially as we ourselves shared them. Nevertheless we hoped that according to our interpretation, for any other interpretation would endanger the basic principle of Provincial autonomy, we might be able to get over some of the obvious difficulties.

But two inseparable obstacles remained, we had hoped that you would be able to remove them. One of these related to the part that European members of the Provincial Assemblies might play in the election to the Constituent Assembly. We have no objection to Englishmen or Europeans as such but we do have a strong objection to persons, who are foreigners and non-nationals and who claim to belong to the ruling race participating in , and influencing the elections to, the Constituent Assembly. The Cabinet Delegations statement lays down clearly that the future Constitution of India has to be decided by Indians. The basic principle of the statement of May 16th was the election of a member of the Constituent Assembly to represent one million inhabitants. On this basis, the representatives of 146,000 Muslims in Orissa and 180,000 Hindus and 58,000 Sikhs in the North-West Frontier Province have not been given the right to elect any member to the Constituent Assembly. The European population in Bengal and Assam numbers only 21,000 but their representatives can return to the Constituent Assembly by their own vote 7 out of 34 members, the appropriating to themselves the right to represent 7 millions. They are to return to the Provincial Assemblies by a separate electorate of their own and have been given fantastic weightage. This representation of European in the Constituent Assembly will be at the cost of non-Muslims, that is mainly Hindus, who are already in minority in Bengal. To make a minority suffer in this way is surely utterly wrong. Apart from the question of Principle, it is a matter of the utmost importance in practice and may well effect the future both of Bengal and Assam. The Congress Working Committee attach the greatest importance to this. We would take to odd that even if the Europeans themselves do not stand for election, but merely vote, the result will be equally bad. The cabinet delegation have informed us that beyond promising of us their persuasive powers they could not hold out any assurance to us that these European members would not exercise the right which, we are advised, they do not possess under the statement of May 16th. But if the Delegation hold otherwise, as evidently they do, we cannot contemplate a legal fight for their exclusion at the threshold of the Constituent Assembly.

Therefore, a clear announcement is necessary that they will not take part as voters or candidates in the election of the Constituent Assembly. We cannot depend on grace or goodwill where rights are concerned.

Equally important, in our view, is the question of 'Parity' in the proposed Provisional National Government. I have already written to you on this subject. This "Parity" or by whatever other name it may be called, has been opposed by us throughout and we consider it a dangerous innovation which, instead of working for harmony, will be a source of continuous conflict and trouble. It may well ...poison our future as other separatist steps in the temporary provision and need not be treated as a precedent, but no such assurance can prevent an evil step from having evil consequences. We are convinced that even the immediate results of any such provision will be harmful.

If the position about the European vote and 'Parity' remains, my Committee are reluctantly compelled to inform you that they will not be able to assist you in the difficult tasks ahead.

The talk we had with you today has not made any substantial difference to the fundamental position. We have noted that, according to your new suggestions, the proposed woman member might be replaced by a Hindu, thus increasing a Hindu members including Scheduled Caste representatives to six. We would be sorry not to have a woman member but apart from this, the new proposal maintains the old Simla (1945) formula of Parity between Caste Hindus and Muslims, with this important qualification that now Muslims are supposed to mean members of the Muslim League. We are unable to agree to the proposal and we are still convinced that the Provisional Government must consist of 15 members and that there should be no kind of Parity in their selection.

Yours sincerely,
A.K. Azad

His Excellency,
Field Marshall Wiscount Wavell,
The Viceroy's House,
New Delhi

Document No. 106

LETTER FROM MAULANA AZAD TO LORD WAVELL

20, Akbar Road,
New Delhi,

14th June, 1946

Confidential

Dear Lord Wavell,

In the course of our talk today you mentioned that among the Muslim League nominees suggested for the Provisional Government was one from the North-West Frontier Province who had recently been defeated at the provincial elections. This was said by you confidentially and we shall of course treat it as such. But I feel I must inform you, do avoid any possibility of misunderstanding that any such name will be considered objectionable by us. The objection is not personal, but we feel that the name is suggested for entirely political reasons and we cannot agree to any such course.

Yours sincerely,
Abul Kalam Azad

His Excellency Field Marshal Viscount Wavell,
Viceroy's House,
New Delhi

Document No. 107

LETTER FROM LORD WAVELL TO MAULANA AZAD

The Viceroy's House,
New Delhi,

14 June, 1946

Confidential

My dear Maulana Saheb,

This is in answer to your confidential letter of June 14th about one of the Muslim League nominees.

I am afraid that I cannot accept the right of the Congress to object to names put forward by the Muslim League, any more than. I would accept similar objections from the other side. The test must be that of ability.

Yours sincerely,
Wavell

Maulana Abul Kalam Azad,
New Delhi

Document No. 108

LETTER FROM LORD WAVELL TO MAULANA AZAD

The Viceroy's House,
New Delhi,
15th June, 1946

My dear Maulana Saheb,

I have received your letter of June 14. I will reply to it in details in the course of today.

Meanwhile I must assume from the last paragraph of your letter that my attempt to negotiate an agreement between the two major parties on the composition of the Interim Government has failed. The Cabinet Delegation and I have therefore decided to issue tomorrow a statement on the action we propose to take; and we will let you have a copy of this before publication.

Yours sincerely,
Wavell

Maulana Abul Kalam Azad,
New Delhi

Document No. 109

LETTER FROM LORD WAVELL TO MAULANA AZAD

Viceroy's House,
New Delhi,
15th June, 1946

My dear Maulana Sahib,

1. I have received your letter of 14th June. You deal with matters on which we have already had much discussion.

2. We are doing everything possible to further the Independence of India. As we have already pointed out however, there must first be a new constitution drawn by the people of India.

3. The delegation and I am aware of your objections to the principle of grouping. I would however, point out that the statement of 16th May does not make grouping compulsory. It leaves the decision to the elected representatives of the provinces concerned sitting together in sections. The only provision which is made is that the representatives of certain Provinces should meet in sections so that they can decide whether or not they wish to form groups. Even when this has been done the individual provinces are still to have the liberty to opt out of the group if they so decide.

4. I recognise the difficulty about the European who through no fault of their own find themselves in a difficult position. I still hope that a satisfactory solution of this problem will be found.

5. Our discussion in regard to the Interim Government have been on the basis of political parties and not communities. I understand that this is regarded as preferable now, as it was at the first Simla Conference. In the proposed Interim Government of myself and 13 others, there will be six Congressmen, and 5 Muslim Leaguers. I do not see how this can be called Parity. Nor there is Parity between Hindus and Muslims, there being six Hindus to five Muslims.

6. Even at this last moment, I still hope that the Congress will now accept the statement and consent to join the Interim Government.

Yours sincerely,
Wavell

Maulana Abul Kalam Azad,
New Delhi

Document No. 110

WORKING COMMITTEE'S RESOLUTION WITH MAULANA AZAD AS PRESIDENT

Resolution on South African Passive Resistance Movement passed by the Congress Working Committee on June 15, 1946.

The Congress Working Committee note with satisfaction not unmixed with concern that Indians in South Africa have started the campaign of civil disobedience as a protest against the recently passed legislation by the South African Union Parliament imposing disabilities upon them. The Congress Working Committee are of opinion that the campaign carries in it the seeds of success in so far as the honour of Indians is concerned as distinguished from the loss of material prospects.

The Committee expect that having begun the struggle the resisters will carry it to the end without yielding. The Committee assure the resisters of full sympathy in their brave struggle and hope that those who are not themselves resisters will not on any account succumb to the temptations contained in the legislation itself and such small concessions that may be held out by the Union Government. The inferior status assigned to the Indians by the Act can be wiped out only by its complete abrogation. The Committee hope and expect that while the Government of India remains in the British Power, His Excellency, the Viceroy will use his influence openly on behalf of the brave resisters and thus secure for them the sympathy of the world in this noble struggle for the rights of man.

Document No. 111

LETTER FROM MAULANA AZAD TO LORD WAVELL

20, Akbar Road,
New Delhi,
16th June, 1946

Dear Lord Wavell,

I have received your two letters of June 15th.

I note what you say about grouping. We abide by our interpretation of it.

As regards European, we are clear that even on a legal interpretation of the statement of May 16th, apart from other considerations, they have not the right to participate .... I am glad you expect a satisfactory solution of this problem.

You have endeavoured in our letter and in the course of talks to state clearly what our position is in regard to a Parity. You will remember that Parity was mentioned and considered at the first Simla Conference. That 'Parity' was exactly the same as is now suggested by you, that is, Parity between Caste Hindus and Muslims. Owing to the stress of War and other conditions then existing, we were prepared to accept this only for that occasion. It was not to be used as a precedent. Moreover, this was subject to the inclusion of at least one Nationalist Muslim. Now conditions have entirely changed and we have to consider the question in an other context, that of approaching, independence and Constituent Assembly. As we have written to you, in this context and in present circumstances we consider this kind of Parity unfair and likely to lead to difficulties. The whole scheme proposed by you in the statement of 16th May is based on absence of weightage. And yet, in the proposed Provisional Government, there is this weightage, in addition to other far-reaching communal safeguards.

We have tried our utmost to arrive at satisfactory settlement and we shall not despair of it. But such a statement, in order to be enduring, must be based on strong foundations. So far as the statement of May 16th is concerned our main difficulty, as we wrote to you, was the European vote. If this matter is settled as now appears likely, then this difficulty also goes.

The second and remaining difficulty relates to the proposals for the provisional government which have to be considered together with the statement. The two cannot be separated. These proposals have thus far been unacceptable to us, but if a satisfactory settlement in this regard to them is arrived at, we would be in a position to shoulder the burden.

Yours sincerely,
A.K. Azad

His Excellency, Field Marshall Viscount Wavell,
The Viceroy's House,
New Delhi

Document No. 112

LETTER FROM LORD WAVELL TO MAULANA AZAD

The Viceroy's House,
New Delhi,

16th June, 1946

Dear Maulana Saheb,

I send herewith a copy of the statement[1] which, as indicated in the letter I sent you yesterday, will be released at 4 P.M. this evening.

As the Statement shows, the Cabinet Ministers and I are fully aware of the difficulties that have prevented an agreement on the composition of the Interim Government. We are unwilling to abandon our hope of a Working Partnership between the two major parties and representatives of minorities. We have therefore done our best to arrive at a practicable agreement taking into consideration the various conflicting claims and the need for obtaining a Government of capable and representative administrator. We hope that the parties will now take their share in the administration of the country on the basis set out in your new statement. We are sure we can rely on you and your Working Committee to look to the wider issues and to the urgent needs of the country as a whole, and to consider this proposal in a spirit of accommodation.

Yours sincerely,
Wavell

Maulana Abul Kalam Azad,
New Delhi

---

1. See Document 113.

Document No. 113

STATEMENT OF THE VICEROY AND THE CABINET MISSION DELEGATION

New Delhi,
16th June, 1946

1. His excellency the Viceroy in consultation with the members of the Cabinet Mission has for some time been exploring the possibilities of forming a coalition Government drawn from the two major parties and certain of the minorities. The discussion have revealed the difficulties which exist for the two major parties in arriving at any agreed basis for the formation of such a Government.

2. The Viceroy and the Cabinet Mission appreciate these difficulties and the efforts which the two parties have made to meet them. They consider however that no useful purpose can be served by further prolonging these discussions. It is indeed urgently necessary that a strong and representative Interim Government should be set up to conduct the very heavy and important business that has to be carried through.

3. The Viceroy is therefore issuing invitation to the following to serve as members of the Interim Government on the basis that the constitution-making will proceed in accordance with the statement of May 16th :

(i) Sardar Baldev Singh,
(ii) Sir N.P. Engineer,
(iii) Mr. Jagjivan Ram,
(iv) Pandit Jawaharlal Nehru,
(v) Mr. M.A. Jinnah,
(vi) Nawabzada Liaquat Ali Khan,
(vii) Mr. C. Rajgopalachari,
(viii) Dr. Rajendra Prasad,
(ix) Mr. H.K. Mehtab,
(x) Dr. John Matthai,
(xi) Nawab Mohammad Ismail Khan,
(xii) Khwaja Sir Nazimuddin,

(xiii) Sardar Abdul Rab Nishtar, and

(xiv) Sardar Vallabhbhai Patel.

If any of these invitations is unable for personal reasons to accept, the Viceroy will, after consultation, invite some other person in his place.

4. The Viceroy will arrange the distribution of portfolios in consultation with the leaders of the two major parties.

5. The above composition of the Interim Government is in no way to be taken as a precedent for the solution of any other communal question. It is an expedient put forward and to solve the present difficulty only, and to obtain the best available coalition Government.

6. The Viceroy and the Cabinet Mission believe that Indians of all communities desire to arrive at a speedy settlement of this matter so that the process of constitution-making can go forward and that the Government of India may be carried on as efficiently as possible in the meantime.

7. They therefore hope that all parties especially the two major parties will accept this proposal so as to overcome the present obstacles, and will co-operate for the successful carrying on of the Interim Government. Should this proposal be accepted, the Viceroy will aim at inaugurating the new Government about the 26th June.

8. In the event of the two major parties on either of them proving, unwilling to join the setting up of a coalition government on the above lines, it is the intention of the Viceroy to proceed with the formation of an Interim Government which will be as representative as possible of those willing to accept the statement of May 16th.

9. The Viceroy is also directing the Governors of Provinces to summon the Provincial Legislative Assemblies forthwith to proceed with the elections necessary for the setting up the constitution-making machinery as put forward in the statement of May 16th.

Document No. 114

LETTER FROM MAULANA AZAD TO LORD WAVELL

20, Akbar Road,
New Delhi,

18th June, 1946

Dear Lord Wavell,

I promised to write to you this evening in case my Committee had come to any decision. The Committee met this afternoon and set for many hours. In the absence of our colleague Abdul Gaffar Khan, who is due to arrive tomorrow morning, we decided to adjourn till tomorrow. I am therefore not in a position this evening to ...convey to you any decision. I shall communicate with you as soon as my Committee arrives at any decision.

Yours sincerely,
A.K. Azad

His Excellency,
Field Marshal Viscount Wavell,
The Viceroy's House,
New Delhi

Document No. 115

LETTER FROM LORD WAVELL TO MAULANA AZAD

The Viceroy's House,
New Delhi,
20th June, 1946

Dear Maulana Sahib,

You will, I am sure, appreciate that the members of the Cabinet Mission have a great deal of urgent work awaiting them in England and are not in a position to prolong their stay in this country indefinitely. I would therefore ask your Working Committee to let us have a final answer as soon as possible to the proposals made in our statement of June 16th.

I understand that you have summoned back the members of the Committee who had left Delhi and in these circumstances we would ask you to let us have your answer not later than Sundy next June 23rd.

Yours sincerely,
Wavell

Maulana Abul Kalam Azad,
New Delhi

Document No. 116

LETTER FROM MAULANA AZAD TO LORD WAVELL

20, Akbar Road,
New Delhi,

21st June, 1946

Dear Lord Wavell,

I have your excellency's letter of 20th June, 1946.

I appreciate your anxiety to come to an early decision regarding the formation of an Interim Government and I can assure you that my Working Committee fully share anxiety. A new difficulty, in addition to the old ones, has however been created by the publication in the press of the alleged contents of Mr. Jinnah's[1] letter to you in which he raises objections to the Congress nominations in the Interim Government. It was to be of great assistance to the Working Committee in coming to a decision if they could have copies of these alleged letters and your reply therefore as they deal with vital matters which we have to consider.

Yours sincerely,
A.K. Azad

His Excellency,
Field Marshall Viscount Wavell,
The Viceroy's House,
New Delhi

1. M.A. Jinnah, first Governor General of Pakistan. Mr. Mohammad Ali Jinnah was the Vice-Chancellor of Osmania University, Supreme Leader of Indian Union Muslim League since 1934, Member Central Legislative Assembly since 1930.

Document No. 117

LETTER FROM LORD WAVELL TO MAULANA AZAD

The Viceroy's House,
New Delhi,
21st June, 1946

Dear Maulana Azad,

Thank you for your letter of today, Mr. Jinnah in his letter to me of the 19th June put to me the following questions:

"(1) Whether the proposals contained in the statement for setting up of an Interim Government are now final or whether they are still open to any further change or modification at the instance of the any parties or persons concerned;

(2) Whether the total number of 14 members of the Government as proposed in the statement would remain unchanged during the Interim period;

(3) If any person or persons invited as representatives of the Four minorities, *viz.*, Scheduled Castes, the Sikhs, the Indian Christians and the Parsis, is or are, unable to accept the invitation to join the Interim Government for personal or other reasons, how will the vacancy or vacancies thus created be filled by the Viceroy; and whether in filling up the vacancy or vacancies the leader of the Muslim League will be consulted and his consent obtained.

(4) (a) Whether during the Interim period for which the coalition Government is being set up the proportion of members of the Government, community-wise, as provided in the proposals, will be maintained;

(b) Whether the present representation given to four minorities, *viz.*, the Scheduled Castes, the Sikhs, the Indian Christians and the Parsis, will be adhered to without any change or of modification; and

(5) In view of the substitution of the new proposal for the original 12, and the change made in the original formula,

whether, there will be a provision, in order to safeguard Muslim interests, that the executive council shall not take any decision or any major communal issue if the majority of the Muslim Members are opposed to it."

2. The operative part of my reply dated the 20th June was as follow:

> "The intention in the statement of June 16 was that the discussion of portfolios with leaders of the two main parties should follow the acceptance by both parties of the scheme. This intention still holds, since until the means are known, it is difficult to decide on the distribution of Portfolios.

On the points which you desire to be made clear in connection with the Government to be formed under our statement of June 16, I give you the following reply after consultation with the Delegation:

> (1) Until I have received acceptance from those invited to take office in the Interim Government, the names in the statement cannot be regarded as final. But no change in the principle will be made in the statement without the consent of the two major parties;
>
> (2) No change in the number of 14 members of the Interim Government will be made without the agreement of the two major parties.
>
> (3) If any vacancy occurs among the seats at present allotted to representatives of minorities, I shall naturally consult both the main parties before filling it;
>
> (4) (a) and (b). The proportion of members by communities will not be changed without the arrangement of the two major parties; and
>
> (5) No decision on a major communal issue could be taken by the Interim Government if the majority of either of the main parties were opposed to it. I pointed this out to the Congress president and he agreed that the Congress appreciated this point.

Yours sincerely,
Wavell

Maulana Abul Kalam Azad
New Delhi

Document No. 118

LETTER FROM LORD WAVELL TO MAULANA AZAD

The Viceroy's House,
New Delhi,

22nd June, 1946

My dear Maulana Saheb,

I understand from press reported that there is a strong feeling in Congress circles that the party should insist on their right to include a Muslim of their choice among the representatives of the Congress in the Interim Government.

For reasons of which you are already aware it is not possible for the Cabinet Mission or myself to accept this request, but I would draw your attention to Paragraph 5 of the statement of the 16th June, which reads as follows:

> The above composition of the Interim Government is in no way to be taken as a precedent for the solution of any other communal question. It is an expedient put forward to solve the present difficulty only and to obtain the best available coalition government.

In the light of this assurance that no precedent is established, we appeal to the Congress not to press their demand but to take part in the strong Interim Government which the country so urgently needs.

Yours sincerely,
Wavell

Maulana Abul Kalam Azad,
New Delhi

Document No. 119

LETTER FROM MAULANA AZAD TO LORD WAVELL

20, Akbar Road,
New Delhi,

24th June, 1946

Dear Lord Wavell,

I have just received the telephone message sent on your behalf asking me to communicate immediately the decision of the Congress Working Committee in regard to the proposals for the Provisional Government. The decision was in fact taken yesterday but we felt that it would be letter if we wrote to you fully on all aspects of the proposals made any you and the Cabinet Delegation. The Working Committee have been sitting almost continuously and will be meeting at 2 P.M. again today. After full consideration and deliberation they have been reluctantly obliged to decide against the acceptance of the Interim Government proposals as framed by you. A detailed and reasoned reply will follow later.

Yours sincerely,
A.K. Azad

His Excellency,
Field Marshal Viscount Wavell,
The Viceroy's House,
New Delhi

Document No. 120

LETTER FROM MAULANA AZAD TO LORD WAVELL

20, Akbar Road,
New Delhi,

25th June, 1946

Dear Lord Wavell,

Ever since receipt of your statement of June 16th, My Committee have been considering it from day to day and have given long and anxious thought to your proposals and to the invitations you have issued to individuals to form the Provisional National Government. Because of our desire to find some way out of the present most unsatisfactory situation, we have tried our utmost to appreciate your approach and viewpoint. In the course of our conversations we have already pointed out to you our difficulties. Unfortunately, these difficulties have been increased by the recent correspondence.

The Congress, as you are aware, is a national organisation including in its fold the member of all religions and communities in India. For more than half a contuny it has laboured for the freedom of India and for equal rights for all Indians. The link that has brought all these various groups and communities together within the fold of the Congress is a passionate desire for national independence, economic advance and social equality. It is from this point of view that we have to judge every proposal. We hoped that a provisional National Government would be formed which would give effect in practice to this independence. Appreciating some of your difficulties, we did not press for any status to my change introducing independence immediately, but we did expect a *de facto* change in the character of the Government making for independence in action. The status and powers of the provisional Government were thus important. In our view this was going to be something entirely different from the Viceroy's executive council. It was to present a new outlook, new method of work and a new psychological approach by India to both domestic and external problems. Your letter dated 30th May, 1946 gave us certain assurances about the status and powers of the Provisional Government. These did not go for enough, according to our thinking but we appreciated the friendly tone of that letter and decided to accept the assurances and not to press this particular matter any further.

The important question of the composition of the Provisional Government remained. In this connection we emphasised that we could not accept anything in the nature of 'Parity' even as a temporary expedient and pointed out that the provisional Government should consist of fifteen members to enable the administration of the country to be carried on efficiently and the smaller minorities to be represented in it. Some mention of names was made and on our part suggestions were put before you informally, including the name of a non-League Muslim.

In your statement of June 16th some of the names suggested came as a surprise tò us. Several changes had been made from the Provisional list prepared by the Congress. The manner of preparing your list and presenting it as an accomplished fact seemed to us to indicate a wrong approach to the problem. One of the names included had not been previously mentioned at all and was that of a person holding an official position and not known to be associated with any public activity. We have no personal objection to him, but we think that the inclusion of such a name particularly without any previous reference or consultation was undesirable and indicated a wrong approach to the problem.

Then again a name from our list was excluded and in his place another of our colleagues was put in, but as you have said that this can be rectified, I need not say more about it.

One outstanding feature of this list was the non-inclusion of any nationalist Muslim. We felt that this was a ... grave omission. We wanted to suggest the name of a Muslim to take the place of one of the Congress names on the list. We felt that no one could possibly object to our changing the name of one of our own men. Indeed when I had drawn your attention to the fact that among the Muslim League nominees was included the name of a person, who had actually lost in the recent elections in the Frontier Province and whose name we felt had been placed there for political reasons. You wrote to me as follows: "I am afraid that I cannot accept the right of the Congress to object to names put forward by the Muslim League any more than. I would accept similar objections from the other side. The test must be that of ability." But before we could make our suggestion I received your letter of the 22nd June which surprised us greatly. You had written this letter on the basis of some press reports. You told us that the Cabinet Mission and you were not prepared to accept a ... request for the inclusion of a Muslim chosen by the Congress among the representatives of the Congress in the Interim Government. This seemed to us an extraordinary decision. It was indirect opposition to your own statement quoted above. It meant that the Congress could not freely choose even its own nominees. The fact that this was not to be taken as a precedent made hardly any difference. Even a temporary departure from such a vital principle could not be accepted by us at any time or place and in any circumstances.

In your letter of the 21st June you gave certain questions framed by Mr. Jinnah in his letter of dated 19th June and your replies to them. We have not seen Mr. Jinnah's letter. In question 3 reference is made to "representation of the four minorities, *viz.*, the Scheduled Castes, the Sikhs, the Indian Christians and the Parsees," and it is asked as to "who will fill in vacancies caused in these groups, and whether in filling up the vacancies the leader of the Muslim League will be consulted and his consent obtained."

In your answer you say: "If any vacancy occurs among the seats at present allotted to representatives of the minorities, I shall naturally consult both the main parties before filling." Mr. Jinnah as thus included the Scheduled Castes among the minorities and presumably you have agreed with this view. So far as we are concerned we repudiate this view and consider the Scheduled Castes as integral part of Hindu society. You also, in your letter of June 15th treated the Scheduled Castes as Hindus. You pointed out that in your proposal there was no 'Parity' either between Hindus and Muslims or between the Congress and the Muslim League in as much as there were to be six Hindus belonging to the Congress, against Five Muslims belonging to the League, one of the six Hindus belonging to the Scheduled Castes. We are in any case not agreeable to the leader of a Party which claims to represent a community which is a minority, interfering with the selection of names from either the Scheduled Castes, whose representation you counted as falling within the Congress quota or with the selection of representatives of the minorities mentioned.

In question 4 the Scheduled Castes are again referred to as a minority and it is asked whether the proportion of members of the Government community-wise as provided in the proposals will be maintained. Your answer is that the proportion will not be changed without agreement of the two major parties. Here again one communal group functioning admittedly as such given a power to veto changes in other groups with ....which it has no concern. We may desire if opportunity offers itself to increase the representation of the Scheduled Castes or to give representation, when it is possible to another minority, for example the Anglo-Indians. All this would depend on the consent of the Muslim League, we cannot agree to this. We may add that your answers restrict the Congress representation to Caste Hindus and make it equal to that of the League.

Finally you state in answer to question 5 that no decision of a major communal issue could be taken by the Interim Government if the majority of either of the main parties were opposed to it. You further say that you had pointed this out to the Congress President and he had agreed that the Congress appreciated this point. In this connection I desire to point out that we had accepted this principle for the long-term arrangement in the Union legislature and it could possibly be applied to the provisional....Government if it was responsible to the legislature and was composed of representatives on the population basis of major communities. It could not be applied to the Provisional Government formed on a different basis altogether. It was pointed out by us in my letter of the 13th June 1946 that it would make administration impossible and deadlocks a certainty. Even in the question as framed by Mr. Jinnah it is stated that "in view of the substitution of 14 now proposed for the original 12" no major communal issues should be decided if the majority of the Muslim Members are opposed to it. Thus this question arose after the substitution of 14 for 12, *i.e.*, after your statement of June 16th. In this statement no mention is made of this rule. This very important change has been introduced, almost casually and certainly without our consent. This again gives the power of veto or obstruction to the Muslim League in the Provisional Government.

We have stated above our....objections to your proposals of June 16th as well as to your answers to the questions framed by Mr. Jinnah[1]. These defects are grave and would render the Working of the Provisional Government difficult and deadlocks a certainty. In the circumstances your proposals cannot fulfil the immediate requirements of the situation or further the cause we hold dear.

My Committee have, therefore, reluctantly come to the conclusion that they are unable to assist you in forming a Provisional Government as proposed in your statement of June 16th, 1946.

1. President of Indian Union Muslim League since 1934. Mr. M.A. Jinnah was elected to the Central Legislative Assembly of India in 1930 and again in 1934. After the division of India he was appointed the first Governor-General of Pakistan.

With regard to the proposals made in the statement of May 16th, 1946 relating to the formation and functions of the constitution-making body, the Working Committee of the Congress passed a resolution on the 24th May, 1946, and conversations and correspondence have taken place between Your Excellency and the Cabinet Mission on the one side and myself and some of my colleagues on the other. In these we have pointed out what in our opinion were the defects in the proposals. We also gave our interpretation of some of the provisions of the statement. While adhering to our views, we accept your proposals and are prepared to work them with a view to achieve our objectives. We would add, however, that the successful working of the Constituent Assembly will largely depend on the formation of a satisfactory Provisional Government.

Yours sincerely,
A.K. Azad

His Excellency,
Field Marshall Viscount Wavell,
The Viceroy's House,
New Delhi

Document No. 121

LETTER FROM LORD WAVELL TO MAULANA AZAD

The Viceroy's House,
New Delhi,

25th June, 1946

Dear Maulana Saheb,

I write to acknowledge receipt of your letter of June 25.

The Cabinet Delegation and I very much regret that the Congress Working Committee have not been able to accept the proposals in the statement of June 16, since, if they had done so. It would have been possible to complete the work to which we and Indian Political leaders have devoted ourselves during the last three months. We are sorry if there was a misunderstanding about the treatment of major communal issues in the Interim Government we certainly thought that you had accepted it as a self evident proposition, as indeed, it is, that in a coalition Government it would not be possible to force through issues of this kind in the face of the opposition of either main parties.

The Delegation and I are, however glad to learn from the last paragraph of your letter that the Congress Working Committee accept, and are prepared to work, the proposals for framing a constitution for India which were put forward in the Delegation's statement of May 16. You say that you adhere to the views and the interpretation of that statement which were set out the Congress Working Committee Resolution of May 24 and in correspondence and interviews with ourselves. At our interview yesterday, we drew your attention to paragraph 8 of our statement of May 25. We emphasised that the procedure for dividing up into sections can only be altered by a resolution of the ... Constituent Assembly passed by a majority 19 (vii) of the statement of May 16.

"We also informed you that in view of the inability of the Congress to co-operate in the Interim Government proposed in our statement of June 16, a situation had arisen in which paragraph 8 of that statement took effect. Accordingly I shall shortly make a further attempt to form an Interim Government as representative as possible of the two main parties. I have, however decided that, as the negotiations have already been protracted and as we have only recently failed to reach agreement it would be desirable to have short interval before the matter is taken up again, and have, therefore, decided to form a Caretaker Government of officials to carry on the administration temporarily.

Yours sincerely,
Wavell

Maulana Abul Kalam Azad,
New Delhi

Appendices

Appendix No. 1

Document No. 122

LETTER FROM MAHATMA GANDHI TO LORD LINLITHGOW

31.12.1942

This is a very personal letter. Contrary to the Biblical injunction I have allowed many suns to set on a quarrel I have harboured against you. But I must not allow the old year to expire without disburdening myself of what is rankling in my breast against you. I have thought we were friends and should still love to think so. However, what has happened since the 9th of August last makes me wonder whether you still regard me as a friend. I have perhaps not come in such close touch with any occupant of your *gadi,* as with you.

Your arrest of me, and the communique you issued threafter, your reply to Rajaji and the reasons given therefor, Mr. Amery's attack on me, and much else I can catalogue, go to show that, at some stage or other, you must have suspected my *bona fides*. Mention of other Congressmen in the same connection is by the way. I seem to be the *fons et origo* of all the evil imputed to the Congress. If I have not ceased to be your friend, why did you not, before taking drastic action, send for me, tell me of your suspicions and make yourself sure of your facts?

I am quite capable of seeing myself as others see me. But in this case I have failed hopelessly. I find that all the statements made about me in Government quarters in this connection contain palpable departures from truth.

I have so much fallen from grace that I could not establish contact with a dying friend. I mean Professor Bhansali who is fasting in regard to the Chimur affair !!!

And I am expected to condemn the so-called violence of some people reputed to be Congressmen, although I have no data for such condemnation save the heavily censored reports of the newspapers. I must own that I thoroughly distrust those reports. I could write much more, but I must not lengthen my tale of woe. I am sure, what I have said is enough to enable you to fill in details.

You know I returned to India from South Africa at the end of 1914 with a mission which came to me in 1906, namely, to spread truth and non-violence among mankind in the place of violence and falsehood in all walks of life. The law of satyagraha knows no defeat. Prison is one of the many ways of spreading the message, but it has its limits. You have placed me in a palace where every reasonable creature comfort is ensured. I have freely partaken of the latter purely as a matter of duty, never as a pleasure, in the hope that some day those who have the power will realize that they have wronged innocent men. I had given myself six months. The law of satyagraha, as I know it, prescribes a remedy in such moments of trial. In a sentence it is, 'Crucify the flesh by fasting.' That same law forbids its use except as a last resort. I do not want to use it, if I can avoid it.

This is a way to avoid it. Convince me of my errors, and I shall make ample amends. You can send for me or send someone who knows your mind and can carry convictions. There are many other ways if you have the will.

May I expect an early reply?

May the New Year bring peace to us all!

Appendix No. 2

Document No. 123

LETTER FROM LORD LINLITHGOW TO MAHATMA GANDHI

January 13, 1943

Thank you for your personal letter of December 31st which I have just received. I fully accept its personal character, and I welcome its frankness. And my reply will be, as you would wish it to be, as frank and as entirely personal as your letter itself.

I was glad to have your letter, for, to be as open with you as our previous relations justify, I have been profoundly depressed during recent months, first, by the policy that was adopted by the Congress in August, secondly, because while that policy gave rise, as it was obvious it must, throughout the country to violence and crime (I say nothing of the risks to India from outside aggression) no word of condemnation for that violence and crime should have come from you or from the Working Committee. When you were first at Poona I know that you were not receiving newspapers, and I accepted that as explaining your silence. When arrangements were made that you and the Working Committee should have such newspapers as you desired, I felt certain that the details newspapers contained of what was happening would shock and distress you, as much as it has us all, and that you would be anxious to make your condemnation of it categorical and widely known. But that was not the case; and it has been a real disappointment to me, all the more when I think of these murders, the burning alive of police officials, the wrecking of trains, the destruction of property, the misleading of these young students, which has done so much harm to India's good name and to the Congress Party. You may take it from me that the newspaper accounts you mention are well founded – I only wish they were not, for the story is a bad one. I well know the immense weight of your great authority in the Congress movement and with the party and those who follow its lead, and I wish I could feel, again speaking very frankly, that a heavy responsibility did not rest on you. (And unhappily, while the initial responsibility rests with the leaders, others have to bear the consequences, whether as law breakers or as the victims.)

But if I am right in reading your letter to mean that in the light of what has happened you wish now to retrace your steps and dissociate yourself from the policy of last summer, you have only to let me know and I will at once consider the matter further. And if I have failed to understand your object, you must not hesitate to let me know without delay in what respect I have done so, and tell me what positive suggestion you wish to put to me. You know me well enough after these many years to believe that I shall be only too concerned to read with the same close attention as ever any message which I receive from you, to give it the fullest weight and to approach it with the deepest anxiety to understand your feelings and your motives.

Appendix No. 3

Document No. 124

LETTER FROM MAHATMA GANDHI TO LORD LINLITHGOW

January 19, 1943

I received your kind letter of 13th instant yesterday at 2.30 p.m. I had almost despaired of ever hearing from you. Please excuse my impatience.

Your letter gladdens me to find that I have not lost caste with you.

My letter of 31st December was a growl against you. Yours is a counter-growl. It means that you maintain that you were right in arresting me and you were sorry for the omissions of which, in your opinion, I was guilty.

The inference you draw from my letter is, I am afraid, not correct. I have re-read my letter in the light of your interpretation, but have failed to find your meaning in it. I wanted to fast and I should still want to, if nothing comes out of our correspondence and I have to be a helpless witness to what is now going on in the country, including the privations of the millions owing to the universal scarcity stalking the land.

If I do not accept your interpretation of my letter, you want me to make a positive suggestion. This, I might be able to do, only if you put me among the members of the Working Committee of the Congress.

If I could be convinced of my error or worse, of which you are evidently, I should need to consult nobody, so far as my own action is concerned, to make a full and open confession and make ample amends. But I have not any conviction of error. I wonder if you saw my letter to the Secretary to the Government of India of 23rd September 1942. I adhere to what I have said in it and in my letter to you of 14th August 1942.

Of course, I deplore the happenings that have taken place since 9th August. But have I not laid the whole blame for them at the door of the Government of India? Moreover, I could not express any opinion on events which I cannot influence or control and of which I have but a one-sided account. You are bound *prima facie* to accept the accuracy of reports that may be placed before you by your departmental heads. But you will not expect me to do so. Such reports have, before now, often proved fallible. It was for that reason that, in my letter of December 31, I pleaded with you to convince me of the correctness of information on which your conviction was based. You will perhaps appreciate my fundamental difficulty in making the statement you have expected me to make.

This, however, I can say from the house-top, that I am as confirmed a believer in no-violence as I have ever been. You may not know that any violence on the part of the Congress workers, I have condemned openly and unequivocally. I have even done public penance more than once. I must not weary you with examples. The point I wish to make is that on every such occasion I was a free man.

This time retracing, as I have submitted, lies with the Government. You will forgive me for expressing an opinion challenging yours. I am certain that nothing but good would have resulted, if you had stayed your hand and granted me the interview which I had announced; on the night of the 8th August, I was to seek. But that was not to be.

Here, may I remind you that the Government of India have before now owned their mistakes, as for instance, in the Punjab when the late General Dyer was condemned, in the U.P. when a corner of a mosque in Cawnpore was restored, and in Bengal when the partition was annulled. All these things were done in spite of great and previous mob violence.

To sum up:

(1) If you want me to act singly, convince me that I was wrong and I will make ample amends.

(2) If you want me to make a proposal on behalf of the Congress you should put me among the Working Committee members.

I plead with you to make up your mind to end the impasse.

If I am obscure or have not answered your letter fully, please point out the omissions and I shall make an attempt to give you satisfaction.

I have no mental reservation.

I find that my letters to you are sent through the Government of Bombay. This procedure must involve some loss of time. As time is of the essence in this matter, perhaps you will issue instructions that my letters to you may be sent directly by the superintendent of this camp.

Appendix No. 4

Document No. 125

LETTER FROM LORD LINLITHGOW TO MAHATMA GANDHI

January 25, 1943

I made clear to you in my last letter that, however reluctantly, the course of events and my familiarity with what has been taking place, has left me no choice but to regard the Congress movement and you as its authorized and fully empowered spokesman at the time of the decision of last August, as responsible for the sad campaign of violence and crime, and revolutionary activity which has done so much harm and so much injury to India's credit since last August. I note what you say about non-violence. I am very glad to read your unequivocal condemnation of violence, and I am well aware of the importance which you have given to that article of your creed in the past. But, the events of these last months, and even the events that are happening today, show that it has not met with the full support of certain, at any rate, of your followers, and the mere fact that they may have fallen short of an ideal which you have advocated is no answer to the relations of those who have lost their lives, and to those themselves who have lost their property or suffered severe injury as a result of violent activities on the part of the Congress and its supporters. And I cannot, I fear, accept as an answer your suggestion that 'the whole blame' has been laid by you yourself at the door of the Government of India. We are dealing with facts in this matter, and they have to be faced. And while, as I made clear in my last letter, I am anxious to have from you anything that you may have to say or any specific proposition that you may have to make, the position remains that it is not the Government of India but Congress and yourself that are on their justification in this matter.

If, therefore, you are anxious to inform me that you repudiate or you dissociate yourself from the resolution of the 9th August and the policy which that resolution represents, and if you can give me the appropriate assurances as regards the future, I shall, I need not say, be very ready to consider the matter further. It is, of course, very necessary to be clear on that point, and you will not, I know, take it amiss that I should make that clear in the plainest possible words.

I will ask the Governor of Bombay to arrange that any communication from you should be sent through him, which will I trust reduce delay in its transmission.

Appendix No. 5

Document No. 126

LETTER FROM MAHATMA GANDHI TO LORD LINLITHGOW

January 29, 1943

I wish I could agree with you that your letter is clear. I am sure you do not wish to imply by clearness simply that you hold a particular opinion strongly. I have pleaded and would continue to plead till the last breath that you should at least make an attempt to convince me of the validity of the opinion you hold that the August resolution of the Congress is responsible for the popular violence that broke out on the 9th of August and after, even though it broke out after the wholesale arrests of principal Congress workers. Was not the drastic and unwarranted action of the Government responsible for the reported violence? You have not even said what part of the August resolution is bad or offensive in your opinion. That resolution is in no way a retraction by the Congress of its policy of non-violence. It is definitely against fascism in every shape or form. It tenders co-operation in the war effort under circumstances which alone can make effective and nation-wide co-operation possible.

The Government have evidently ignored or overlooked the very material fact that the Congress, by its August resolution, asked nothing for itself. All its demands were for the whole people. As you should be aware, the Congress was willing and was prepared for the Government inviting Qaid-e-Azam Jinnah to form a national government, subject to such agreed adjustments as may be necessary for the duration of war, such government being responsible to a duly elected assembly. Being isolated from the Working Committee, except Shrimati Sarojini Devi, I do not know its present mind. But the committee is not likely to have changed its mind.

Is all this open to reproach?

Objection may be raised to that clause of the resolution which contemplated civil disobedience. But that by itself cannot constitute an objection, since the principle of civil disobedience is impliedly conceded in what is known as 'Gandhi-Irwin Pact.' Even that civil disobedience was not to be started before knowing the result of the meeting for which I was to seek from you an appointment.

'Then, take the unproved and, in my opinion, the unprovable charges hurled against the Congress and me by so responsible a minister as the Secretary of State for India.

Surely I can say with safety that it is for the Government to justify their action by solid evidence, not by mere *ipse dixit*.

But you throw in my face the facts of murders by persons reputed to be Congressmen. I see the fact of the murders as clearly, I hope, as you do. My answer is that the Government goaded the people to the point of madness. They started leonine violence in the shape of the arrests already referred to. That violence is not any the less so, because it is organized on a scale so gigantic that it displaces the Mosaic law of tooth for tooth by that of ten thousand for one – not to mention the corollary of the Mosaic law, that is, of non-resistance as enunciated by Jesus Christ. I cannot interpret in any other manner the repressive measures of the all-powerful Government of India.

Add to this tale of woe, the privations of the poor millions due to India-wide scarcity which I cannot help thinking might have been largely mitigated, if not altogether prevented, had there been a *bona fide* national government responsible to a popularly elected assembly.

If then I cannot get soothing balm for my pain, I must resort to the law prescribed for the satyagrahis, namely, a fast according to capacity. I must commence after the early morning breakfast of the 9th February a fast for twenty-one days, ending on the morning of the 2nd March. Usually, during my fasts, I take water with the addition of salts. But nowadays my system refuses water. This time, therefore, I propose to add juices of citrus fruits to make the water drinkable. For, my wish is not to fast unto death, but to survive the ordeal, if God so wills. The fast can be ended sooner by the Government giving the needed relief.

I am not marking this letter personal, as I did the two previous ones. They were in no way confidential. They were mere personal appeal.

Appendix No. 6

Document No. 127

LETTER FROM LORD LINLITHGOW TO MAHATMA GANDHI

February 5, 1943

In my last letter I said that my knowledge of the facts left me no choice but to regard the Congress movement and you as its authorized and fully empowered leader at the time of decision of last August, as responsible for the campaign of violence and crime that subsequently broke out. In reply, you have reiterated your request that I should attempt to convince you that my opinion is correct. I would readily have responded earlier to that request, were it not that your letters gave no indication such as I should have been entitled to expect, that you sought the information with an open mind. In each of them you have expressed profound distrust of the published reports of the recent happenings, although in your last letter, on the basis of the same information, you have not hesitated to lay the whole blame for them on the Government of India. In the same letter you have stated that I cannot expect you to accept the accuracy of the official reports on which I rely. It is not, therefore, clear to me how you expect or even desire me to convince you of anything. But in fact, the Government of India have never made any secret of their reasons for holding the Congress and its leaders responsible for the deplorable acts of violence and sabotage and terrorism that have occurred since the Congress Resolution of the 8th August declared a 'mass struggle' in support of its demands, appointed you as its leader and authorized all Congressmen to act for themselves in the event of interference with the leadership of the movement. A body which passes a resolution in such terms is hardly entitled to disclaim responsibility for any events that follow it. There is evidence that you and your friends expected this policy to lead to violence; that you were prepared to condone it; and that the violence that ensued formed part of a concerted plan, conceived long before the arrest of the Congress leaders. General nature of the case against the Congress has been publicly stated by the Home Member in his speech in the Central Legislative Assembly on 15th September last, and if you need further information I would refer you to it. I enclose a complete copy in case the press versions that you must have seen were not sufficient. I need only add that all the mass of evidence that has come to light has confirmed the conclusions then reached. And I have ample information that the campaign of sabotage has been conducted under secret instructions, circulated in the name of the A.I.C.C.; that well-known Congressmen have organized and freely taken part in acts of violence and murder; and that even now an underground Congress organization exists in which, among others, the wife of a member of the Congress Working Committee plays a prominent part, and which is actively engaged in planning the bomb outrages and other acts of terrorism that have disgusted the whole country. If we do not act on all this information or make it publicly known, it is because the time is not yet ripe; but you may rest assured that the charges against the Congress will have to be met sooner or later and it will then be for you and your colleagues to clear yourselves before the world, if you can. And if in the meanwhile you yourself, by any action such as you now appear to be contemplating, attempt to find an easy way out, the judgement will go against you by default.

I have read with surprise your statement that the principle of civil disobedience is implicitly conceded in the Delhi settlement of 1931, which you refer to as Gandhi-Irwin Pact. I have again looked at the document. Its basis was that civil disobedience would be 'effectively discontinued' and certain 'reciprocal action' would be taken by the Government. It was inherent in such a document that it should take notice of the existence of civil disobedience. But, I can find nothing in it to suggest that civil disobedience was recognized as being in any circumstances legitimate. And I cannot make it too plain that it is not so regarded by my Government.

To accept the point of view which you put forward would be to concede that the authorized Government of the country, on which lies the responsibility for maintaining peace and good order, should allow subversive and revolutionary movements described by you yourself as open rebellion to take place unchallenged; that they should allow preparations for violence, for interruptions of communications, for attacks on innocent persons, for murder of police officers and others to proceed unchecked. My Government and I are open, indeed, to the charge that we should have taken drastic action at an earlier stage against you and Congress leaders. But my anxiety and that of my Government has throughout been to give you, and to give the Congress organization, every possible opportunity to withdraw from the position which you have decided to take up. Your statements of last June and July, the original resolution of the Working Committee of July 14, and your declaration on the same day that there was no room left for negotiation, and that after all it was an open rebellion are all of them grave and significant, even without your final exhortation to 'do or die.' But with a patience that was perhaps misplaced, it was decided to wait until the resolution of the A.I.C.C. made it clear that there could be no further toleration of the Congress attitude if Government was to discharge its responsibility to the Indian people.

Let me in conclusion say how greatly I regret, having regard to your health and age, the decision that you tell me that you now have in your mind to take. I hope and pray that wiser counsels may yet prevail with you. But the decision whether or not to undertake a fast with its attendant risks is clearly one that must be taken by you alone and the responsibility for which and for its consequences must rest on you alone. I trust sincerely that in the light of what I have said you may think better of your resolution and I would welcome a decision on your part to think better of it, not only because of my own natural reluctance to see you wilfully risk your life, but because I regard the use of a fast for political purposes as a form of political blackmail (*himsa*) for which there can be no moral justification, and understood from your own previous writings that this was also your view.

Appendix No. 7

Document No. 128

LETTER FROM MAHATMA GANDHI TO LORD LINLITHGOW

February 7, 1943

I would take your last point first, namely, the contemplated fast which begins on the 9th instant. Your letter, from a satyagrahi's standpoint, is an invitation to fast. No doubt the responsibility for the step and its consequences will be solely mine. You have allowed an expression to slip from your pen for which I was unprepared. In the concluding sentence of the second paragraph, you describe the step as an attempt 'to find an easy way out'. That you, as a friend, can impute such a base and cowardly motive to me passes comprehension. You have also described it as 'a form of political blackmail', and you quote my previous writings on the subject against me. I abide by my writings. I hold there is nothing inconsistent in them with the contemplated step. I wonder whether you have yourself read those writings.

I do claim that I approached you with an open mind when I asked you to convince me of my error. A 'profound distrust' of the published reports is in no way inconsistent with my having an open mind.

You say that there is evidence that I (I leave my friends out for the moment) 'expected this policy to lead to violence', that I was 'prepared to condone it,' and that 'the violence that ensued formed part of a concerted plan conceived long before the arrest of Congress leaders.' I have seen no evidence in support of such a serious charge. You admit that part of the evidence has yet to be published. The speech of the Home Member, of which you have favoured me with a copy, may be taken as the opening speech of the prosecution counsel and nothing more. It contains unsupported imputations against Congressmen. Of course, he has described the violent outburst in graphic language. But he has not said why it took place when it did. I have suggested why it did. You have condemned men and women before trying them and hearing their defence. Surely, there was nothing wrong in my asking you to show me the evidence on which you hold them guilty. What you say in your letter carries no conviction. Proof should correspond to the canons of English jurisprudence.

If the wife of a member of the Congress Working Committee is actively engaged in 'planning the bomb outrages and other acts of terrorism,' she should be tried before a court of law and punished if found guilty. The lady you refer to could only have done the things attributed to her after the wholesale arrests of 9th August last which I have dared to describe as leonine violence.

You say that the time is not yet ripe to publish the charges against the Congress. Have you ever thought of the possibility of their being found baseless when they are put before an impartial tribunal, or that some of the condemned persons might have died in the meanwhile, or that some of the evidence that the living can produce might become unavailable?

I reiterate the statement that the principle of civil disobedience is implicitly conceded in the settlement of the 5th March 1931, arrived at between the then Viceroy on behalf of the Government of India and myself on behalf of the Congress. I hope you know that the principal Congressmen were discharged before that settlement was even thought of. Certain reparations were made to the Congressmen under that settlement. Civil disobedience was discontinued only on conditions being fulfilled by the Government. That by itself was, in my opinion, an acknowledgement of its legitimacy, of course, under given circumstances. It, therefore, seems somewhat strange to find you maintain that civil disobedience 'cannot be recognized as being in any circumstances legitimate by your Government.' You ignore the practice of the British Government which has recognized its legitimacy under the name of 'passive resistance.'

Lastly, you read into my letters a meaning which is wholly inconsistent with my declaration in one of them, of my adherence to unadulterated non-violence. For, you say in your letter under reply, that 'acceptance of my point of view would be to concede that the authorized Government of the country on which lies the responsibility for maintaining peace and good order, would allow the movements to take place that would admit preparations for violence, interruptions of communications, for attacks on innocent persons, for murders of police officers and others, to proceed unchecked.' I must be a strange friend of yours, whom you believe to be capable of asking for recognition of such things as lawful.

I have not attempted an exhaustive reply to the views and the statements attributed to me. This is neither the place nor the time for such reply. I have only picked out those things which in my opinion demanded an immediate answer. You have left me no loophole for escaping the ordeal I have set before for myself. I begin it on the 9th instant with the clearest possible conscience. Despite your description of it as 'a form of political blackmail', it is on my part meant to be an appeal to the Highest Tribunal for justice which I have failed to secure from you. If I do not survive the ordeal, I shall go to the Judgement Seat with the fullest faith in my innocence. Posterity will judge between you as representative of an all-powerful Government and me as a humble man who had tried to serve his country and humanity through it.

Appendix No. 8

Document No. 129

LETTER FROM THE HOME SECRETARY OF INDIA TO MAHATMA GANDHI

February 8, 1943

The Government of India would be very reluctant to see you fast, and I am instructed to inform you that they would propose that, should you persist in your intention, you will be set at liberty for the purpose and for the duration of your fast as from the time of its commencement. During the period of your fast, there will be no objection to your proceeding where you wish, though the Government of India trust that you will be able to arrange for your accommodation away from Aga Khan Palace.

"Should you for any reason find yourself unable to take advantage of the arrangements, a decision which the Government of India would greatly regret, they will of course suitably amend the statement of which a copy is now enclosed before it issues. But they wish to repeat, with earnestness, their anxiety and their hope that the considerations which have carried so much weight with them will equally carry weight with you, and that you will not pursue your present tentative proposal."

Appendix No. 9

Document No. 130

LETTER FROM MAHATMA GANDHI TO THE HOME SECRETARY, GOVERNMENT OF INDIA

February 9, 1943

I have very carefully studied your letter. And I am sorry to say that there is nothing in the correspondence which has taken place between His Excellency and myself or your letter to warrant a recalling of my intention to fast. I have mentioned in my letters to His Excellency the conditions which can induce the prevention or suspension of the step.

If the temporary release is offered for my convenience, I do not need it. I should be quite content to take my fast as a detenu or prisoner. If it is for convenience of the Government I am sorry I am unable to suit them much as I should like to do so. I can say this much that I, as a prisoner, shall avoid, as far as is humanly possible, every cause of inconvenience to the Government, save what is inherent in the fast itself. The impending fast has not been conceived to be taken as a free man. Circumstances may arise, as they have done before now, when I may have to fast as a free man. If, therefore, I am released, there will be no fast in terms of my correspondence above mentioned. I shall have to survey the situation *de novo* and decide what I should do. I have no desire to be released under false pretences. In spite of all that has been said against me, I have not to believ the vow of truth and non-violence which alone makes life livable for me. I say this, if it is only for my own satisfaction. It does me good to reiterate openly my faith, when outer darkness surrounds me, as it does just now.

I must not hustle the Government into a decision on this letter. I understand that your letter has been dictated through telephone. In order to give the Government enough time, I shall suspend the fast, if necessary, to Wednesday next, 10th instant.

So far as the statement proposed to be issued by the Government is concerned, and of which you have favoured me with a copy, I can have no opinion. But if I might have I must say that it does me an injustice. The proper course would be to publish the full correspondence and let the public judge for themselves.

Appendix No. 10

Document No. 131

MESSAGE FROM THE GOVERNMENT OF INDIA FOR MAHATMA GANDHI

February 9, 1943

The Government of India note your decision with great regret. Their position remains the same, that is to say, they are ready to set you at liberty for the purpose and duration of your fast. But, if you are not prepared to take advantage of that fact and if you fast while in detention, you will do so solely on your own responsibility and at your own risk. In that event, you will be at liberty to have your own medical attendants, and to receive visits from friends with the permission of Government during its period. Suitable drafting alterations will be made in the statement which the Government of India would, in that event, issue to the press.

Appendix No. 11

Document No. 132

OFFICIAL ANNOUNCEMENT IN CONNECTION WITH THE FAST BY MAHATMA GANDHI

February 10, 1943

Mr. Gandhi had informed H.E. the Viceroy that he proposes to undertake a fast of three weeks' duration from 10th February. It is to be a fast according to capacity, and during it Mr. Gandhi proposes to add juices of citrus fruit to water to make water drinkable, as his wish is not to fast to death, but to survive the ordeal. The Government of India deplore the use of the weapon of fasting to achieve political ends. There can, in their judgement, be no justification for it, and Mr. Gandhi has himself admitted in the past that it contains an element of coercion. The Government of India can only express its regret that Mr. Gandhi should think it necessary to employ such a weapon on this occasion, and should seek a justification for it in anything which Government may have said or done in connection with the movement initiated by him and his co-workers in the Congress Party. The Government of India have no intention on their part of allowing the fast to deflect their policy. Nor will they be responsible for its consequences on Mr. Gandhi's health. They cannot prevent Mr. Gandhi from fasting. It was their wish, however, that if he decided to do so, he should do so as a free man and under his own arrangements, so as to bring out clearly that the responsibility for any fast and its consequences rested exclusively with him. They accordingly informed Mr. Gandhi that he would be released for the purpose and for the duration of the fast of which he had notified them, and with him any members of the party living with him who may wish to accompany him. In reply Mr. Gandhi has expressed his readiness to abandon his intended fast if released, failing which he will fast in detention. In other words, it is now clear that only his unconditional release would prevent him from fasting. This the Government of India are not prepared to concede. Their position remains the same: that is to say, they are ready to set Mr. Gandhi at liberty for the purpose and duration of his fast. But if Mr. Gandhi is not prepared to take advantage of that fact and if he fasts while in detention, he does so solely on his own responsibility and at his own risk. He would be at liberty in that event to have his own medical attendants, and also to receive visits from friends with the permission of Government during its period.

The Government of India propose to issue, in due course, a full statement on the origin and development of the movement which was initiated in August last, and measures Government have been compelled to adopt to deal with it. But they think this a suitable occasion for a brief review of the events of the last few months.

Mr. Gandhi, in his correspondence with the Viceroy, has repudiated all responsibility for the consequences which have flowed from the 'Quit India' demand which he and the Congress Party have put forward. This contention will not bear examination. Mr. Gandhi's own statement, before the movement was launched, envisaged anarchy as an alternative to the existing order, and referred to the struggle as 'a fight to the finish in the course of which he would not hesitate to run any risk, however great.' As much has been made of his offer to meet the Viceroy, it is necessary to point out that a press interview on the 14th of July, after the Working Committee Resolution was passed, Mr. Gandhi stated that there was no room left in the proposal for withdrawal or for negotiation; there was no question on one more chance; it was an open rebellion which was to be as short and as swift as possible. His last message was 'do or die'. The speeches of those most closely associated with Mr. Gandhi have been even more explicit and have given a clear indication of what the Congress High Command had in mind in launching their attack – an attack which would, if realized, have most seriously imperilled the whole cause of the United Nations – against Government by law established, and against the agencies and services by which the life of the country was being conducted in a period, be it noted, of exceptional stress and strain, and of grave danger to India from Japanese aggression.

The instructions issued by the various Congress organizations contained in the leaflets which were found to be freely circulating in almost every part of India – and which, on the evidence, cannot all be disowned as unauthorized – gave specific directions bringing the administration to a standstill. The circular of the 29th July emanating from the Andhra Provincial Congress Committee is an instance in point. It is noteworthy in this connection that in the widely separated areas all over the country identical methods of attacks on the railways and other communications were employed, requiring the use of special implements and highly technical knowledge. The control rooms and block instruments in railway stations came in for special attention and the destruction of telegraph and telephone wires and equipment was carried out in a manner which denoted a careful planning and a close knowledge of their working. If these manifestations of the rebellious activities are to be regarded as the result not of Congress teachings but as a manifestation of popular resentment against the arrest of Mr. Gandhi and the Congress leaders, the question may well be asked to which section of the public the tens of thousands of men engaged in these violent subversive activities belonged. If it is claimed that it is not the Congressmen who have been responsible, then it would be extraordinary, to say the least, if the blame were to be laid on non-Congress elements. The country is, in effect, asked to believe that those who own allegiance to the Congress Party have behaved in an exemplary non-violent manner, and that it is persons who are outside the Congress fold who have registered their resentment at the arrest of the leaders of a movement which they did not profess to follow. A more direct answer to the argument is to be had in the fact that known Congressmen have been repeatedly found engaged in incitements to violence, or in prosecuting the Congress activities which have led to grave disorders.

That the political parties and groups outside the Congress Party have no delusions on the subject may be judged from the categorical way in which they have dissociated themselves from the movement and condemned the violence to which it has given rise. In particular the Muslim League has, on more than one occasion, emphasized the character and the intentions of the policy pursued by the Congress Party. As early as the 20th of August last, the Working Committee of the League expressed the view, reiterated many times since, that by the slogan 'Quit India' what was really meant was supreme control of the government of the country by the Congress, and that the mass civil disobedience movement had resulted in lawlessness and considerable destruction of life and property. The other elements in the political life of the country have expressed themselves in a similar vein, and if the followers of the Congress persist in their contention that the resultant violence was no part of their policy or programme, they are doing so against the weight of the overwhelming evidence.

Mr. Gandhi in his letter to the Viceroy has sought to fasten responsibility on the Government of India. The Government of India emphatically repudiate the suggestion. It is clearly preposterous to contend that it is they who are responsible for the violence of the last few months, which so gravely disorganized the normal life of the country and, incidentally, aggravated the difficulties of the food situation at a time when the united energies of the vital task of repelling the enemy and striking a blow for the freedom of India, the commonwealth and the world.

Appendix No. 12

Document No. 133

RESOLUTION PASSED BY THE COUNCIL OF THE ALL INDIA MUSLIM LEAGUE ON 6TH JUNE 1946

1. This meeting of the Council of the All India Muslim League, after having carefully considered the Statement issued by the Cabinet Mission and the Viceroy on 16th May 1946, and other relevant statements and documents officially issued in connection therewith, and after having examined the proposals set forth in the said Statement in all their bearings and implications, places upon record the following views for the guidance of the Nation and direction to the Working Committee.

2. That the references made, and the conclusions recorded, in paras 6,7,8,9,10 and 11 of the Statement, concerning the Muslim demand for the establishment of a full sovereign Pakistan as the only solution of the Indian constitutional problem are unwarranted, unjustified, and unconvincing, and should not therefore have found a place in a state document issued on behalf and with the authority of the British Government. These paragraphs are couched in such language, and contain such mutilations of the established facts that the Cabinet Mission have clearly been prompted to include them in their Statement solely with the object of appeasing the Hindus, in utter disregard of Muslim sentiments. Furthermore, the contents of the aforesaid paragraphs are in conflict and inconsistent with the admissions made by the Mission themselves in paras 5 and 12 of their Statement, which are to the following effect: First, the Mission "were greatly impressed by the very genuine and acute anxiety of the Muslims lest they should find themselves subjected to a perpetual Hindu majority rule." Second, "This feeling has become so strong and widespread amongst the Muslims that it cannot be allayed by mere paper safeguards." Third, "if there is to be internal peace in India it must be secured by measures which will assure to the Muslims a control in all matters vital to their culture, religion, economic or other interests." Fourth, "Very real Muslim apprehensions exist that their culture and political and social life might become submerged

in a purely unitary India, in which the Hindus, with their greatly superior numbers, must be the dominating element." In order that there may be no manner of doubt in any quarter, the Council of the All India Muslim League reiterates that the attainment of the goal of a complete sovereign Pakistan still remains the unalterable objective of the Muslims in India for the achievement of which they will, if necessary, employ every means in their power, and consider no sacrifice or suffering too great.

3. That notwithstanding the affront offered to Muslim sentiments by the choice of injudicious words in the preamble to the Statement of the Cabinet Mission, the Muslim League, having regard to the grave issues involved, and prompted by its earnest desire for a peaceful solution, if possible, of the Indian constitutional problem, and inasmuch as the basis and the foundation of Pakistan are inherent in the Mission's plan by virtue of the compulsory grouping of the six Muslim Provinces in Sections B and C, is willing to cooperate with the constitution-making machinery proposed in the scheme outlined by the Mission, in the hope that it would ultimately result in the establishment of complete sovereign Pakistan, and in the consummation of the goal of independence for the major nations, Muslims and Hindus, and all the other people inhabiting the vast subcontinent.

It is for these reasons that the Muslim League is accepting the scheme, and will join the constitution-making body, and it will keep in view the opportunity and right of secession of Provinces or groups from the Union, which have been provided in the Mission's plan by implication. The ultimate attitude of the Muslim League will depend on the final outcome of the labours of the constitution-making body, and on the final shape of the constitutions which may emerge from the deliberations of that body jointly and separately in its three sections. The Muslim League also reserves the right to modify and revise the policy and attitude set forth in this resolution at any time during the progress of the deliberations of the constitution-making body, or the Constituent Assembly, or thereafter if the course of events so require, bearing in mind the fundamental principles and ideals herebefore adumbrated, to which the Muslim League is irrevocably committed.

4. That with regard to the arrangement for the proposed Interim Government at the Centre, this Council authorizes its President to negotiate with the Viceroy and to take such decisions and actions as he deems fit and proper.

Who's Who

Abdullah, Sheikh Muhammad	:	A prominent leader of Kashmir Valley, was sent to jail in 1946 by Maharaja; became the head of the Government of State of Jammu and Kashmir (1947) and the Premier since 1948.
Anney, M.S.	:	Reputed national leader, some time member of Viceroy's Council; was the president of first session of All India Hindu League, held at Lucknow in 1935.
Anugraha, Narayan Sinha	:	A leading Congressman of Bihar, Finance Minister in the Cabinet of Shrikrishna Sinha in 1946.
Asaf Ali	:	A prominent Congress leader of Delhi, was appointed a Minister in Interim Government in 1946.
Azad, Maulana Abul Kalam	:	A Great Freedom Fighter and Editor of *Al-Hilal, Al-Balagh* and the *Vakil of Amritsar*, was elected President of Indian National Congress in 1940 at Wardha; was appointed first Education Minister in Free India's Cabinet.
Bajaj, Jamna Lal	:	Prominent Congress leader of Central Provinces and industrialist, president Charkha Sangh and treasurer of A.I.C.C., took active part in the Nagpur Flag Satyagraha in 1923.
Bardoloi, Gopinath	:	Prominent Congress leader of Assam, became the Premier of the State in 1937 and Chief Minister in 1946.

Basu, J.N.	: A liberal leader of Bengal and the member of State Legislative Council (1934-36).
Birla, G.D.	: Well known industrialist and a devotee of Mahatma Gandhi, was the President of Harijan Sewak Sangh, became member of Central Legislative Assembly.
Bose, Sarat Chandra	: Prominent Congress leader of Bengal and elder brotheer of Netaji Subash Chander Bose. He was a member of Interim Government, headed by Pandit Nehru in 1946.
Bose, Subas Chandra	: Great patriot and front ranking Congress leader of Bengal, elected President of Indian National Congress twice in 1938 at Haripura and in 1939 at Tripuri, founder of Forward Bloc (1939), Indian National Army and Indian National Government during the Second World War, imprisoned several times during National Liberational Movement.
Chatterji, B.C.	: A great poet, patriot and Member of the Legislative Council of Bengal (1934-36)
Chowdhary, Khaliquzama	: A Prominent leader of United Provinces Muslim League; was elected to U.P. Legislative Assembly in 1937.
Das, Nilakantha	: A leading Congressman of Orissa.
Das, Biswanath	: Leader of Orissa Congress Legislative Party and the Premier of the state in 1937.
Deo, Shankarrao	: A front ranking Congress leader of Maharashtra, was appointed a member to the Working Committee of Indian National Congress by Maulana Azad in 1940.
Desai, Bhulabhai J.	: A prominent Congress leader and well-known Advocate of Bombay, Leader of Congress Party in Central Legislative

		Assembly (1946). Marvellusly pleaded for I.N.A. convicts (1946). His Party's with Liyakat Ali Khan when Congress leaders were in Jail regarding the future set-up of national government had been one of the reasons for Congress which commends core attitude towards him. A nearest friend of Maulana Azad.
Deshmukh, R.M.	:	Chief Minister of Vindhya Pradesh (1947-50).
Diwakar, R.R.	:	Well-known Congress leader of Karnataka; was appointed a Minister of State in Central Government in 1948.
Gadgil, N.V.	:	A prominent Congress leader of Maharashtra; was appointed a Minister in Union Cabinet by Nehruji.
Gandhi, Devadas	:	Youngest son of Mahatma Gandhi and son-in-law of C. Rajgopalachari; was the Managing Editor of *The Hindustan Times.*
Gandhi, M.K.	:	Supreme Leader of National Liberation Movement and Indian National Congress (1920-47), President of I.N.C. (1925), Editor of *Young India* and *Navjeevan* (1920-31), *Harijan Bandhu* and *Harijan Sewak* (1933-42), participated in the Second Round Table Conference held in London in 1931.
Gidwani, Choithram	:	A Congress leader of Sind; President of S.P.C.C. before independence.
Gilani, B.S.	:	Private Secretary to Sardar Baldev Singh and a Spokesman of Christians.
Ghose, P.C.	:	A Congress leader of Bengal, was the Chief Minister of West Bengal before Dr. B.C. Roy.
Gupta, J.M. Sen	:	A prominent Congressman of Bengal and social worker.
Haq, A.J. Fazlul	:	Leader, Krishak Praja Party of Bengal and the Chief Minister.

Hasan, S.M. : A member in the Central Provinces Ministry in 1937 and again in 1946.

Humayun Kabir : A close associate of Maulana Azad, was appointed a State Minister in Union Government in 1959.

Jairamdas Daulatram : Congress leader of Sind, member Working Committee (1940-46); Minister in the Union Cabinet, headed by Pt. Nehru in 1947.

Jinnah, M.A. : Vice-Chancellor of Osmania University, Supreme Leader of Muslim League since 1934, Member, Indian Legislative Assembly (1924-34), first Governor General of Pakistan.

Khan, Abul Gaffar Khan : Frontier Gandhi and Organiser of Khudai Khidmatgar in N.W.F.P; started Red Shirt Movement in the Province (1930); member, Congress Working Committee from 1936-47.

Khan Saheb, Dr. : Elder brother of Frontier Gandhi and a leading Congressman, became the Premier of N.W.F.P. in 1946.

Khare, N.B. : Premier of Central Provinces in 1937.

Kidwai, Rafi Ahmed : Prominent Congress leader of U.P.; a nearest friend of Pandit Nehru; became a member in the Union Cabinet in 1952.

Kripalani, J.B. : A front ranking Congress leader; was appointed the Principal of Gujarat Vidyapeeth; imprisoned several times during the National Liberation Movement; elected President to the Meerut Session of I.N.C. in 1946.

Lal, Sir Manohar : A leading member of Unionist Party and Finance Minister of Punjab before partition.

Liaquat Aki Khan : Prominent leader of U.P. Muslim League, leader Muslim League Parliamentary Party (1946); became the first Prime Minister of Pakistan in 1947.

Lawrence, Sir Pathick	: A Senior British Statesman; was a member of Cabinet Mission Plan sent to India by the British Government in 1946; was appointed Secretary of State for India in 1945 in place of Amery.
Madni, Hussain Ahmed	: President Jamiat-Ulema-i-Hind and noted scholar of Islamic Philosophy; founder of Darul Ulum, Deoband and a nearest friend of Maulana Azad.
Maitra, Pandit Lakshmi	: A member of Indian Legislative Assembly (1934-37).
Mahtab, H.K.	: Veteran freedom fighter and Congress leader of Orissa; was the Chief Minister of the State from 1946 to 1950.
Misra, Chintamani	: Congressman and Journalist of Orissa.
Misra, D.P.	: Leading Congressman of Central Provinces, Minister in the State Government in 1937 and again in 1946.
Mufti, Kifaytullah	: Scholar and freedom fighter of U.P.
Munshi, K.M.	: A well-known barrister and Congress leader of Bombay; was appointed Agent General by Government of India in Hyderabad State in 1948.
Navalrai, Lal Chand	:. A member of Indian Legislative Assembly (1934-37).
Naidu, Sarojini	: Top ranking Congress worker of Hyderabad; was elected President of Indian National Congress (1926); became the first Governor of U.P. after independence.
Narayan, J.P.	: Founder Secretary of the Socialist Party of India and a noted freedom fighter.
Narayan Ram	: Famous Congress Worker of Bihar; was an associate of Dr. Rajendra Prasad.
Nariman, K.F.	: President of Bombay Provincial Congress Committee (1934-37); was prevented to become the leader of C.L.P.B. in 1937 due to his anti-party activities in the elections of 1934.

Nawab Ismail Khan : Leader of U.P. Muslim League; was elected to the State Assembly in 1937 and again in 1946.

Nehru, Jawaharlal : A leading figure of National Liberation Movement, was elected President of Indian National Congress in 1929, 1936, 1937 and 1946; founder All India Kisan Sabha, Bharat Krishak Samaj and the President of States People Organisation; became the first Prime Minister of India after independence in 1947.

Nehru, Motilal : Famous barrister of Allahabad and a front ranking Congress leader, was elected President of Indian National Congress in 1919 and again in 1928.

Nehru, Swaroop Rani : Wife of Pandit Motilal Nehru and the mother of Pandit Jawaharlal Nehru.

Pandit, Vijaya Lakshmi : Younger sister of Pandit Jawaharlal Nehru, was elected to the Legislative Assembly of U.P. (1937); became the Chairperson of the General Assembly of U.N.O; was appointed Indian Ambassador to Soviet Union.

I aliwal, Shrikrishna Dutta: A leading Congress worker of U.P.

Pant, G.B. : Front ranking Congress leader of U.P.; became the premier of the State in 1937 and the Chief Minister in 1946, elected to the Working Committee of I.N.C. several times between 1936 and 1950; was appointed Home Minister in the Union Cabinet headed by Pandit Nehru.

Patel, Manibehn : Famous social worker and freedom fighter; became the member of Congress Working Committee in 1950, was elected to the Indian Parliament several times between 1952 and 1980. She was the daughter of Sardar Vallabhbhai Patel.

Patel, Vallabhbhai : Popularly known as Sardar; was the organiser of Bardoli Peasant Agitation (1928), elected President of Indian

	National Congress at Karachi in 1931, became the Chairman of C.P.B. in 1934 and 1936, appointed Deputy Prime Minister of free India in 1947.
Patel, Vithalbhai	: Front ranking Congress leader of Bombay; was the Barrister of B.H.C.; elected to the L.C.B. in 1913; became Chairman, B.M.C. in 1924; elected President of the Indian Legislative Assembly in 1925.
Prakasham, T.	: Leading Congressman of Andhra Pradesh, became the Chief Minister of State in 1946.
Patwardhan, Achyut	: Noted freedom fighter and Socialist Party's leader.
Prasad, Rajendra	: Top-ranking Congress leader and constructive worker of Bihar; was a colleague of Maulana Azad, Sardar Patel and Pandit Nehru and associate of Mahatma Gandhi; elected President of Indian National Congress (1935); became a member Congress Parliamentary Board (1937); appointed Food and Civil Supplies Minister in the interim Government (1946), elected Chairman Constituent Assembly (1946) and the President of Indian Republic in 1950, 1952 and 1957.
Rajgopalacharier, C.	: Gandhian thinker and front ranking Congressman of Madras, became twice Chief Minister of the province; was the first and last Indian Governor-General (1948-50), appointed Minister for Home Affairs in the Government of India in 1950, Well-known for his suave diplomacy and cruditeness; founder of Swatantra Party of India.
Ray, B.C.	: Renowned doctor and Congress leader of Bengal, become the Chief Minister of W.B. in 1939.

Ray, M.N.	: Well-known thinker and freedom fighter of Bengal, praticipated in Communist International, held in Moscow in 1920; was defeated by Maulana Azad in the election of Congress Presidentship at Wardha in 1940.
Sachchar, Bhim Sen	: Prominent Congress leader of Punjab, became a Secretary of P.C.C. in 1921, was elected to State Legislative Assembly in 1936 and 1945; Chief Minister of Punjab in 1952-56.
Sahai, K.B.	: A Parliamentary Secretary in Bihar Ministry 1937.
Sahjanand, Swamy	: Leading public leader of Bihar and the founder of All India Kisan Sabha.
Sadulla, Muhammad	: Leader of Assam Muslim League; became Premier of the State in 1939.
Sanskrityayan, Rahul	: A noted freedom fighter and progressive writer.
Shah, Shantilal Harjivan Lal	: Constructive worker of Gujarat; was a founder member of Indian National Trade Union Congress and incharge of Congress Election Office in 1945-46.
Saksena, Mohan Lal	: A member of Indian Legislative Assembly (1934-37).
Shareef, M.	: A Minister in the Central Provinces Government in (1937-38), headed by Dr. N.B. Khare.
Sherwani, T.A.K.	: A Prominent Zamindar and Congressman of U.P.; was elected President of U.P.P.C.C. in 1929; a nearest friend of Pandit Nehru and Kisan Leader.
Silva, George Da	: Leading Congressman and the Vice-President of Mahakoshal Provincial Congress Committee.
Sinha, Shrikrishna	: A well-known Congress leader of Bihar; became the Chief Minister of the Province.

Syed, G.M.	: A Leading Muslim Leader of Sind.
Sitaramayya, B. Pattabhi	: Leading Congressman of Andhra; was elected President of Indian National Congress in 1948.
Sriprakasha	: Congress leader of U.P.; appointed Indian High Commissioner to Pakistan (1947); became Governor of Assam in 1945.
Sukhla, R.S.	: A leading Congressman and the Premier of the Central Provinces (1938-39); Pandit Ravi Shankar Shukla was again elected as leader of C.P.C.L.P. in 1946.
Tagore, Rabindra Nath	: Great Bengali Poet as well as the Philosopher; was the founder of Vishwa Bharti University of Shantiniketan. A Nobel Prize Winner, Social Reformer and the Author of the "Geetanjali".
Tara Singh, Master	: Akali Leader of Punjab who started agitation for a separate Sikh State.

Glossary

Ahimsa	:	Non-Violence
Akali Dal	:	Religious and Political Organization of the Sikhs.
All India Spiners Association	:	An All India body, formed by Gandhiji in 1925 to provide employement to the starving millions of India.
Bapu	:	Literally father a generic term to denote respect to elder, a term widely used by Indian people for Gandhiji.
Civil Disobedience Movement	:	Non-Violent or Satyagraha Movement of Mahatma Gandhi to resist British Rule in India.
Charkha	:	Spinning wheel.
Constructive Programme	:	Mahatma Gandhi's eighteen point programme for India's resurgence.
Dharma	:	Religion
Gurudwara	:	Worship place of Sikhs
Harijan	:	The term used by Mahatma Gandhi for the people belonging to Scheduled Castes of India; a weekly started by Gandhiji from 1933.
Individual Satyagraha	:	Mahatma Gandhi's campaign of 1940 through satyagrahis of his choice to protest against Britain's war-effort in India.
Khadi	:	Hand-spun and hand-woven cloth.
Lahore Resolution	:	A resolution passed by All India Muslim League in March, 1940 at Lahore, under the Presidentship of

		Mr. Mohammad Ali Jinnah, to launch an agitation to get India divided into two nations.
Mahatma	:	A title bestowed on Gandhiji by Dr. Rabindra Nath Tagore.
Non-Violence	:	Ahimsa which along with truth and love formed the *summum bonum* of the philosophical view of Mahatma Gandhi's positive force to resist tyranny and injustice.
Qaumi Ekta	:	National Unity.
Quit India Movement	:	Started by Mahatma Gandhi on August 9, 1942 to force the Britain to Quit India. Gandhiji, by starting the movement, appealled the people to adopt any means to fight against the evil designs of imperialistic government which were ruthlessly suppressing people.
Quit India Resolution	:	A resolution adopted by the All India Congress Committee in Bombay on 8 August, 1942, under the presidentship of Maulana Abul Kalam Azad to force the British to withdraw from India.
Rajaji Formula	:	A formula popularly known as 'Rajaji Formula' put forward by Chakravarty Rajgopalacharier in connection with the working arrangement with the Muslim League. Rajaji had developed a Conviction that only division of the country was the appropriate political solution for the constitutional problem of India.
Ram Raj	:	The rule of God, Mahatma Gandhi's conception on ideal non-exploitative human society wedded to truth, love, non-violence, brotherhood and communal harmony.
Sardar	:	Leader or captain, a title bestowed on Vallabhbhai Patel by Mahatma Gandhi in 1928 after the victory of Bardoli Kisan Satyagraha.
Satyagraha	:	Literally insistance on truth, Mahatma Gandhi's weapon of truth and love (with non-violence) for mass action.
Satyagrahi	:	A believer of Satyagraha.

Swaraj : Self Rule or complete independence.
Zamindar : Landlord.
Zamindari : Landlordism.
Zulum : Atrocities.

Chronology of Events
(1943-46)

1943,	March	15	: President of Akali Dal suggested Maulana Azad to consult Sikhs at every stage of any communal settlement.
	April	9	: Wife Begam Zulaikha Khatoon died.
	June		: Younger sister Hanifa Begum Abru died at Bhopal.
1945	April	16	: Transferred to Bankura from Ahmed Nagar Fort.
	June	15	: Released from Bankura Jail after 1,040 days of imprisonment.
	June	16	: Participated in Simla Conference along with other Indian leaders and talked with Viceroy Lord Wavell which failed due to Mr. Jinnah's insistence to accept Muslim representatives nominated by Muslim League only.
	June	20	: Congress Committee authorised Azad to accept the invitation of Viceroy for further talk in Simla on 22.6.45.
			: Took over responsibility as Chairman for elections to Central and Provincial Legislative Assemblies.
	July	9	: Included Master Tara Singh's name in list of members for Viceroy's Council.
1946			: Ghubar-i-Khatir and Karwan-i-Khayal published.
			: Talked with the Cabinet Mission at Simla.
	June	15	: C.W.C. passed a resolution on South African Passive Resistance Movement with Maulana Azad as President.
	June	16	: The Viceroy and the Cabinet Mission Delegation issued a Statement after long-term talks with Indian leaders.

Index

B

C

D

E

L

M

N